Annual Report
on
Exchange Arrangements
and Exchange Restrictions
2013

CD-ROM Edition including Overview

International Monetary Fund

©2013 International Monetary Fund

Cataloging-in-Publication Data
Joint Bank-Fund Library

Assessing macroprudential policies in a financial stability framework. –
Washington, D.C. : International Monetary Fund, 2013.
   p. ; cm.

Special topic of the Annual report on exchange arrangements and exchange
restrictions, 2013 issue.

   Includes bibliographical references.
   ISBN: 978-1-48436-680-6 (Print)
   ISBN: 978-1-47555-261-4 (PDF)
   ISBN: 978-1-48435-431-5 (ePub)
   ISBN: 978-1-47557-805-8 (Mobi)

1.   Financial institutions – State supervision. 2. Financial crises - Prevention.
         I. International Monetary Fund.

HG173.A87 2013

ISSN (Online) 2304-0831
ISSN (Print) 0250-7366

Please send orders to:
International Monetary Fund, Publication Services
P.O. Box 92780, Washington, D.C. 20090, U.S.A.
Tel.: (202) 623-7430 Fax: (202) 623-7201
E-mail: publications@imf.org
www.imfbookstore.org

Contents

Country Chapters on CD-ROM[1]

Afghanistan	Djibouti
Albania	Dominica
Algeria	Dominican Republic
Angola	Ecuador
Antigua and Barbuda	Egypt
Argentina	El Salvador
Armenia	Equatorial Guinea
Aruba	Eritrea
Australia	Estonia
Austria	Ethiopia
Azerbaijan	Fiji
The Bahamas	Finland
Bahrain	France
Bangladesh	Gabon
Barbados	The Gambia
Belarus	Georgia
Belgium	Germany
Belize	Ghana
Benin	Greece
Bhutan	Grenada
Bolivia	Guatemala
Bosnia and Herzegovina	Guinea
Botswana	Guinea-Bissau
Brazil	Guyana
Brunei Darussalam	Haiti
Bulgaria	Honduras
Burkina Faso	Hong Kong Special Administrative Region
Burundi	Hungary
Cambodia	Iceland
Cameroon	India
Canada	Indonesia
Cape Verde	Islamic Republic of Iran
Central African Republic	Iraq
Chad	Ireland
Chile	Israel
China	Italy
Colombia	Jamaica
Comoros	Japan
Democratic Republic of the Congo (DRC)	Jordan
Republic of Congo (Congo)	Kazakhstan
Costa Rica	Kenya
Côte d'Ivoire	Kiribati
Croatia	Korea
Curaçao and Sint Maarten	Kosovo
Cyprus	Kuwait
Czech Republic	Kyrgyz Republic
Denmark	Lao People's Democratic Republic

---

[1] The term "country," as used in this publication, does not in all cases refer to a territorial entity that is a state as understood by international law and practice; the term also covers some territorial entities that are not states but for which statistical data are maintained and provided internationally on a separate and independent basis.

Latvia
Lebanon
Lesotho
Liberia
Libya
Lithuania
Luxembourg
Former Yugoslav Republic of Macedonia
Madagascar
Malawi
Malaysia
Maldives
Mali
Malta
Marshall Islands
Mauritania
Mauritius
Mexico
Micronesia
Moldova
Mongolia
Montenegro
Morocco
Mozambique
Myanmar
Namibia
Nepal
Netherlands
New Zealand
Nicaragua
Niger
Nigeria
Norway
Oman
Pakistan
Palau
Panama
Papua New Guinea
Paraguay
Peru
Philippines
Poland
Portugal
Qatar
Romania
Russia
Rwanda
St. Kitts and Nevis
St. Lucia

St. Vincent and the Grenadines
Samoa
San Marino
São Tomé and Príncipe
Saudi Arabia
Senegal
Serbia
Seychelles
Sierra Leone
Singapore
Slovak Republic
Slovenia
Solomon Islands
Somalia
South Africa
South Sudan
Spain
Sri Lanka
Sudan
Suriname
Swaziland
Sweden
Switzerland
Syria
Tajikistan
Tanzania
Thailand
Timor-Leste
Togo
Tonga
Trinidad and Tobago
Tunisia
Turkey
Turkmenistan
Tuvalu
Uganda
Ukraine
United Arab Emirates
United Kingdom
United States
Uruguay
Uzbekistan
Vanuatu
Venezuela
Vietnam
Yemen
Zambia
Zimbabwe

Preface

The *Annual Report on Exchange Arrangements and Exchange Restrictions* has been published by the IMF since 1950. It draws on information available to the IMF from a number of sources, including information provided in the course of official staff visits to member countries, and has been prepared in close consultation with national authorities.

This project was coordinated in the Monetary and Capital Markets Department by a staff team directed by Karl F. Habermeier and comprising Chikako Baba, Roy Baban, Ricardo Cervantes, Salim Darbar, Mehmet Ziya Gorpe, Ivett Jamborne, and Annamaria Kokenyne. It draws on the specialized contribution of that department (for specific countries), with assistance from staff members of the IMF's five area departments, together with staff of other departments. John Gregg Forte drafted the Special Topic. The report was edited and produced by Linda Griffin Kean of the Communications Department with assistance from Lucy Scott Morales.

Abbreviations

AANZFTA	ASEAN–Australia–New Zealand Free Trade Agreement
ACU	Asian Clearing Union (Bangladesh, Bhutan, India, Islamic Republic of Iran, Maldives, Myanmar, Nepal, Pakistan, Sri Lanka)
AD	Authorized dealer
AFTA	ASEAN Free Trade Area (see ASEAN, below)
AGOA	African Growth and Opportunity Act (United States)
AMU	Asian monetary unit
ASEAN	Association of Southeast Asian Nations (Brunei Darussalam, Cambodia, Indonesia, Lao P.D.R., Malaysia, Myanmar, Philippines, Singapore, Thailand, Vietnam)
BCEAO	Central Bank of West African States (Benin, Burkina Faso, Côte d'Ivoire, Guinea-Bissau, Mali, Niger, Senegal, Togo)
BEAC	Bank of Central African States (Cameroon, Central African Republic, Chad, Republic of Congo, Equatorial Guinea, Gabon)
CACM	Central American Common Market (Belize, Costa Rica, Dominican Republic, El Salvador, Guatemala, Honduras, Nicaragua)
CAEMC	Central African Economic and Monetary Community (members of the BEAC)
CAFTA	Central American Free Trade Agreement
CAP	Common agricultural policy (of the EU)
CARICOM	Caribbean Community and Common Market (Antigua and Barbuda, Barbados, Belize, Dominica, Grenada, Guyana, Haiti, Jamaica, Montserrat, St. Kitts and Nevis, St. Lucia, St. Vincent and the Grenadines, Suriname, Trinidad and Tobago); The Bahamas is also a member of CARICOM, but it does not participate in the Common Market
CB	Central bank
CEFTA	Central European Free Trade Area (Bulgaria, Hungary, Poland, Romania, Slovak Republic, Slovenia)
CEPGL	Economic Community of the Great Lakes Countries (Burundi, Democratic Republic of the Congo, Rwanda)
CET	Common external tariff
CFA	Communauté financière d'Afrique (administered by the BCEAO) and Coopération financière en Afrique centrale (administered by the BEAC)
CIMA Code	Chartered Institute of Management Accountants Code of Ethics for Professional Accountants
CIS	Commonwealth of Independent States (Armenia, Azerbaijan, Belarus, Georgia, Kazakhstan, Kyrgyz Republic, Moldova, Russia, Tajikistan, Turkmenistan, Ukraine, Uzbekistan)
CITES	Convention on International Trade in Endangered Species of Wild Fauna and Flora
CMA	Common Monetary Area (a single exchange control territory comprising Lesotho, Namibia, South Africa, and Swaziland)
CMEA	Council for Mutual Economic Assistance (dissolved; formerly Bulgaria, Cuba, Czechoslovakia, German Democratic Republic, Hungary, Mongolia, Poland, Romania, U.S.S.R., Vietnam)

Note: This list does not include acronyms of purely national institutions mentioned in the country chapters.

COMESA	Common Market for Eastern and Southern Africa (Burundi, Comoros, Democratic Republic of the Congo, Djibouti, Egypt, Eritrea, Ethiopia, Kenya, Madagascar, Malawi, Mauritius, Namibia, Rwanda, Seychelles, Sudan, Swaziland, Uganda, Zambia, Zimbabwe)
EAC	East African Community
EBRD	European Bank for Reconstruction and Development
EC	European Council (Council of the European Union)
ECB	European Central Bank
ECCB	Eastern Caribbean Central Bank (Anguilla, Antigua and Barbuda, Dominica, Grenada, Montserrat, St. Kitts and Nevis, St. Lucia, St. Vincent and the Grenadines)
ECCU	Eastern Caribbean Currency Union
ECOWAS	Economic Community of West African States (Benin, Burkina Faso, Cape Verde, Côte d'Ivoire, The Gambia, Ghana, Guinea, Guinea-Bissau, Liberia, Mali, Niger, Nigeria, Senegal, Sierra Leone, Togo)
ECSC	European Coal and Steel Community
EEA	European Economic Area
EFSF	European Financial Stability Facility
EFSM	European Financial Stability Mechanism
EFTA	European Free Trade Association (Iceland, Liechtenstein, Norway, Switzerland)
EIB	European Investment Bank
EMU	European Economic and Monetary Union (Austria, Belgium, Cyprus, Estonia, Finland, France, Germany, Greece, Ireland, Italy, Luxembourg, Malta, Netherlands, Portugal, Slovak Republic, Slovenia, Spain)
EPZ	Export processing zone
ERM	Exchange rate mechanism (of the European monetary system)
EU	European Union (formerly European Community); Austria, Belgium, Bulgaria, Croatia, Cyprus, Czech Republic, Denmark, Estonia, Finland, France, Germany, Greece, Hungary, Ireland, Italy, Latvia, Lithuania, Luxembourg, Malta, Netherlands, Poland, Portugal, Romania, Slovak Republic, Slovenia, Spain, Sweden, United Kingdom)
FATF	Financial Action Task Force on Money Laundering (of the OECD)
FDI	Foreign direct investment
FEC	Foreign exchange certificate
FSU	Former Soviet Union
G7	Group of Seven advanced economies (Canada, France, Germany, Italy, Japan, United Kingdom, United States)
GAFTA	Greater Arab Free Trade Agreement
GCC	Gulf Cooperation Council (Cooperation Council for the Arab States of the Gulf; Bahrain, Kuwait, Oman, Qatar, Saudi Arabia, United Arab Emirates)
GSP	Generalized System of Preferences
IBRD	International Bank for Reconstruction and Development (World Bank)
IMF	International Monetary Fund
LAIA	Latin American Integration Association (Argentina, Bolivia, Brazil, Chile, Colombia, Ecuador, Mexico, Paraguay, Peru, Uruguay, Venezuela)
LC	Letter of credit
LIBID	London interbank bid rate

LIBOR	London interbank offered rate
MERCOSUR	Southern Cone Common Market (Argentina, Brazil, Paraguay, Uruguay, Venezuela)
MFN	Most favored nation
MOF	Ministry of finance
NAFTA	North American Free Trade Agreement
OECD	Organization for Economic Cooperation and Development
OECS	Organization of Eastern Caribbean States (Antigua and Barbuda, Dominica, Grenada, Montserrat, St. Kitts and Nevis, St. Lucia, St. Vincent and the Grenadines)
OGL	Open general license
OTC	Over the counter
PACER	Pacific Agreement on Closer Economic Relations (of the Pacific Islands Forum; Australia, Cook Islands, Fiji, Kiribati, Marshall Islands, Micronesia, Nauru, New Zealand, Niue, Palau, Papua New Guinea, Samoa, Solomon Islands, Tonga, Tuvalu, Vanuatu)
PICTA	Pacific Island Countries Trade Agreement (of the Pacific Islands Forum); Cook Islands, Fiji, Kiribati, Marshall Islands, Micronesia, Nauru, Niue, Palau, Papua New Guinea, Samoa, Solomon Islands, Tonga, Tuvalu, Vanuatu)
RCPSFM	Regional Council on Public Savings and Financial Markets (an institution of WAEMU countries that is involved in issuance and marketing of securities authorization)
RIFF	Regional Integration Facilitation Forum (formerly Cross-Border Initiative); Burundi, Comoros, Kenya, Madagascar, Malawi, Mauritius, Namibia, Rwanda, Seychelles, Swaziland, Tanzania, Uganda, Zambia, Zimbabwe)
SACU	Southern African Customs Union (Botswana, Lesotho, Namibia, South Africa, Swaziland)
SADC	Southern Africa Development Community (Angola, Botswana, Democratic Republic of the Congo, Lesotho, Malawi, Mauritius, Mozambique, Namibia, Seychelles, South Africa, Swaziland, Tanzania, Zambia, Zimbabwe)
SDR	Special drawing right
UCITS	Undertakings for the Collective Investment of Transferable Securities
UDEAC	Central African Customs and Economic Union (Cameroon, Central African Republic, Chad, Republic of Congo, Equatorial Guinea, Gabon)
UN	United Nations
UNSC	UN Security Council
VAT	Value-added tax
WAEMU	West African Economic and Monetary Union (formerly WAMU; members of the BCEAO)
WAMA	West African Monetary Agency (formerly WACH)
WAMZ	West African Monetary Zone
W-ERM II	Exchange rate mechanism (of the WAMZ)
WTO	World Trade Organization

Overview

This volume (64th issue) of the *Annual Report on Exchange Arrangements and Exchange Restrictions* (AREAER) provides a description of the foreign exchange arrangements, exchange and trade systems, and capital controls of all IMF member countries.[1] The AREAER reports on restrictions in effect under Article XIV, Section 2, of the IMF's Articles of Agreement in accordance with Section 3 of Article XIV, which mandates annual reports on such restrictions. It also provides information related to Paragraph 25 of the 2012 Integrated Surveillance Decision, which restates the obligation under the IMF's Articles of Agreement of each member country to notify the IMF of the exchange arrangement it intends to apply and any changes in the arrangement.[2]

The AREAER endeavors to provide a comprehensive description of exchange and trade systems, going beyond exchange restrictions or exchange controls. In addition to information related to restrictions on current international payments and transfers and multiple currency practices (MCPs) maintained under Article XIV of the IMF's Articles of Agreement, it includes restrictions and MCPs subject to the IMF's jurisdiction in accordance with Article VIII, Sections 2(a) and 3.[3] The report also provides information on the operation of foreign exchange markets and controls on international trade. It describes controls on capital transactions and measures implemented in the financial sector, including prudential measures. In addition, it reports on exchange measures imposed by member countries for security reasons, including those notified to the IMF in accordance with relevant decisions by the IMF Executive Board.[4]

This report provides detailed information on the de jure and de facto exchange rate arrangements of member countries. The de jure arrangements are reported as described by the countries. The de facto exchange rate arrangements are classified into 10 categories.[5] The classification is based on the information available on members' de facto arrangements, as analyzed by the IMF staff, which may differ from countries' officially announced (de jure) arrangements. The methodology and the characteristics of the categories are described in the Compilation Guide.[6]

The AREAER aims to provide timely information. In general, the report includes a description of exchange and trade systems as of December 31, 2012. However, changes in member countries' exchange rate arrangements are reflected as of April 30, 2013, and in some cases, reference is made to other significant developments through August 31, 2013.[7]

---

[1] In addition to the 188 IMF member countries, the report includes information on Hong Kong SAR (China) as well as Aruba and Curaçao and Sint Maarten (all Netherlands).

[2] www.imf.org/external/np/sec/pn/2012/pn1289.htm.

[3] The information on restrictions and MCPs consists of verbatim quotes from each country's most recent published IMF staff report as of December 31, 2012, and represents the views of the IMF staff, which may not necessarily have been endorsed by the IMF Executive Board. In cases of unpublished IMF staff reports, the quotes have been included verbatim in the AREAER with the express consent of the member country. In the absence of such consent, the relevant information is reported as "not publicly available." If countries implement changes to these restrictions and MCPs after the relevant IMF report has been issued, these changes will be reflected in a subsequent issue of the AREAER, covering the year during which the IMF staff report with information on such changes is issued.

[4] The information on exchange measures imposed for security reasons is based solely on information provided by country authorities.

[5] The categories of exchange rate arrangements are (1) hard pegs comprising (a) exchange arrangements with no separate legal tender and (b) currency board arrangements; (2) soft pegs consisting of (a) conventional pegged arrangements, (b) pegged exchange rates within horizontal bands, (c) crawling pegs, (d) stabilized arrangements, and (e) crawl-like arrangements; (3) floating regimes, under which the exchange rate is market determined and characterized as (a) floating or (b) free floating; and (4) a residual category, other managed arrangements. These categories are based on the flexibility of the arrangement and the way it operates in practice—that is, the de facto regime is described, rather than the de jure or official description of the arrangement.

[6] Effective February 2, 2009, the classification methodology was revised to allow for greater consistency and objectivity of classifications across countries and improved transparency, in the context of the IMF's bilateral and multilateral surveillance.

[7] The date of the most recent reported development is indicated in the detailed information for each country included in the country chapters on the CD enclosed with the printed Overview and in the AREAER Online database.

To facilitate easy comparison, a single table provides an overview of the characteristics of the exchange and trade systems of all IMF member countries (see the Summary Features of Exchange Arrangements and Regulatory Frameworks for Current and Capital Transactions in IMF Member Countries). The Country Table Matrix lists the categories used in the database, and the Compilation Guide includes definitions and explanations used by member countries to report the data and for use in interpreting this report.

The AREAER is available in several formats. This Overview of the year's developments is available in print and online, and detailed information for the 191 countries and territories covered here is included on a CD that accompanies the printed Overview and in an online database, AREAER Online. In addition to the information on the exchange and trade systems of these 191 countries and territories in 2012, AREAER Online contains historical data published in previous issues of the AREAER. It is searchable by year, country, and category of measure and allows cross-country comparisons for time series.[8]

Overall Developments during 2012

The general trend toward foreign exchange liberalization and strengthening the financial sector regulatory framework continued during 2012 against a backdrop of slow recovery from the global crisis and an incomplete transition to financial stability. Financial and market conditions improved markedly starting in late 2012, but global economic conditions remained subdued amid changing dynamics that point to stronger underlying activity in advanced economies and slowing growth in major emerging market economies. Accommodative monetary policy in advanced economies helped boost growth pulled down by fiscal consolidation and a still weak financial system but also contributed to capital outflows to emerging market economies during most of the reporting period. Changes in investor sentiment increased the volatility of capital flows to emerging market economies and led to the large-scale pullout of investments from emerging market economies following the announcement in May by the Federal Reserve that a tapering of U.S. monetary easing would begin in the second half of 2013. Improved market conditions allowed a return to more stable exchange rate regimes and facilitated the easing of controls on current and capital transactions, but concerns about capital flow volatility may have motivated the tightening of capital controls and the imposition of restrictions in selected countries. There was continued reform of financial sector regulatory frameworks, with countries further strengthening financial regulations in recognition of the vulnerabilities that contributed to the global financial crisis.

The 2013 AREAER documents the following major trends and significant developments:

- Improved market conditions and slowly recovering growth may have facilitated the reversal of the shift toward more flexible exchange rates evident during the previous reporting period. The number of countries that used a soft peg bounced back almost to its previous (April 2011) level while the number that fell into the residual category—other managed arrangements—experienced the greatest decline. In short, countries returned to more stable exchange rate arrangements they had previously abandoned because of weakening external balance positions or strong appreciation pressure.

- The exchange rate remained the anchor for monetary policy for fewer than half of member countries, which increasingly opted to monitor multiple indicators. The U.S. dollar maintained its position as the dominant exchange rate anchor and increased its share when new member South Sudan adopted this framework. This followed a steady five-year decline in the number of countries using the U.S. dollar as exchange rate anchor.

- In contrast to the previous reporting period, the major advanced economies reported no exchange rate interventions. This was not the case for some smaller advanced economies and emerging market economies, which have experienced mounting pressure on their exchange rates against the backdrop of increased capital flow volatility. Their heightened intervention activity was evident in self-reporting, various market reports, and significant changes in some members' foreign exchange reserves.

---

[8] For further information on these resources, see www.imfbookstore.org or www.elibrary.imf.org.

- Continuing the trend during 2011, there was increased use during 2012 and early 2013 of foreign exchange auctions to facilitate foreign exchange operations in less-developed foreign exchange markets as a tool for managing foreign reserves and as a vehicle for foreign exchange interventions.

- Changes in forward transactions gravitated toward easing, both to roll back measures introduced during the crisis and as part of a broader liberalization process. Taxes on foreign exchange transactions were generally tightened to address pressure on exchange rates, but decreasing capital inflows prompted some reduction in tax rates.

- The number of IMF member countries accepting the obligations of Article VIII, Sections 2(a), 3, and 4, remained 168 with no new acceptances. When South Sudan became a member in April 2012, it notified the IMF that it avails itself of transitional arrangements under Article XIV with respect to measures under IMF jurisdiction in effect on the date of its membership. This raised the number of Article XIV members to 20.

- The trend continued toward greater current account openness despite the weakness of the global recovery. The regulatory framework eased considerably for exports and imports and for current invisible transactions, notwithstanding some tightening of the norms on current account transactions and a slight increase in exchange restrictions motivated by external imbalances and macro-financial considerations. This was particularly the case for the repatriation and surrender of export proceeds and for import procedures, suggesting that countries are increasingly relying on the external trade channel to boost growth. Unlike in 2011, there was an increase in the total number of exchange restrictions on current payments and transfers in 2012 as well as in the number of members maintaining them.

- Developments in 2012 and early 2013 were shaped by members' continued efforts to strengthen the financial regulatory framework, concerns about financial stability, and volatile capital flows. There was a continuation of the overall trend toward liberalization of capital transactions except in the financial sector. Most of the countries carried out gradual liberalization or rolled back controls introduced at the height of the global crisis, but others used capital controls to respond to the changing global environment, in particular to increased capital flow volatility. Specifically, there was a return of investors to emerging markets at the end of 2012, but flows began to shifting toward advanced economies in the early part of 2013 with improved U.S. growth prospects, new progrowth policies in Japan, weaker growth prospects in emerging markets, and fears about an early tapering of U.S. monetary stimulus. Although most of the measures introduced in the reporting period affected cross-border lending, the liberalization trend was most pronounced in foreign direct investment.

- The prudential framework of banks' operations continued to strengthen, as it has since the global crisis, although the pace slowed somewhat. In addition, the changes that occurred in capital controls tightened existing norms on commercial banks and other credit institutions, which suggests that in some countries concerns about financial stability may be significant enough to require tools stronger than just nondiscriminatory prudential measures. Reported changes easing prudential frameworks in the financial sector were mostly aimed at supporting the restructuring and recovery of the banking sector; many rolled back previous tightening and expanded institutional investors' investment opportunities. A large share of the measures affecting reserve requirements attests to the importance of this tool in the pursuit of monetary policy and financial stability objectives and in the response to changes in capital flows. As in the previous year, the framework for commercial banks' foreign exchange risk management was overwhelmingly tightened, likely reflecting concerns about risks related to increased variability in foreign exchange markets.

The remainder of this Overview highlights the major developments covered in this issue of the AREAER. Details of member countries' exchange arrangements and their regulatory frameworks for current and capital transactions are presented in the individual country chapters, which are available on the CD that accompanies the printed Overview or through AREAER Online.

Developments in Exchange Arrangements

This section documents major changes and trends in the following related areas: exchange rate arrangements, intervention, monetary anchors, and the operation and structure of foreign exchange markets. It also reports on significant developments with respect to exchange taxes, exchange rate structures, and national currencies. There are nine tables within this section. Table 1 summarizes the detailed descriptions in the country chapters by reporting each IMF member country's monetary policy framework as indicated by country officials and the classification of their de facto exchange rate arrangements. Table 2 breaks down countries' de facto exchange rate arrangements for 2008–13. Table 3 highlights changes in the reclassification of the de facto exchange rate arrangements between January 1, 2012, and April 30, 2013. Table 4 outlines IMF member countries' monetary anchors, and Table 5 reports other changes related to the exchange rate and monetary policy frameworks. Table 6 presents the structure of the foreign exchange markets among the membership, and Table 7.a reports changes regarding foreign exchange markets. Last, Tables 7.b and 7.c report changes in currency and exchange rate structures and exchange subsidies and taxes, respectively.

Exchange Rate Arrangements

Improved market conditions may have contributed to the almost complete reversal of the previous shift to more flexible exchange rate arrangements. After losing about 4 percent of member countries during the period January 2011–April 2012, the soft peg category strengthened almost to its previous (April 2011) level, reaching 42.9 percent of the membership (see Table 2). This change further widened the gap between soft pegs and floating arrangements. Countries with soft pegs represent the single largest exchange rate arrangement category—almost equal to the combined number of floating and other managed arrangements (44 percent of members). More specifically, both the stabilized and crawl-like arrangement categories expanded, while the residual other managed arrangement category contracted markedly.

- There were no changes between April 2012 and April 2013 among the countries that have no separate legal tender or currency boards. In fact, the countries with these arrangements tend to maintain their exchange rate policies unless there are large structural changes in their economies.

Table 1. De Facto Classification of Exchange Rate Arrangements and Monetary Policy Frameworks, April 30, 2013

The classification system is based on the members' actual, de facto arrangements as identified by IMF staff, which may differ from their officially announced, de jure arrangements. The system classifies exchange rate arrangements primarily on the basis of the degree to which the exchange rate is determined by the market rather than by official action, with market-determined rates being on the whole more flexible. The system distinguishes among four major categories: hard pegs (such as exchange arrangements with no separate legal tender and currency board arrangements); soft pegs (including conventional pegged arrangements, pegged exchange rates within horizontal bands, crawling pegs, stabilized arrangements, and crawl-like arrangements); floating regimes (such as floating and free floating); and a residual category, other managed.

This table presents members' exchange rate arrangements against alternative monetary policy frameworks in order to highlight the role of the exchange rate in broad economic policy and illustrate that different exchange rate regimes can be consistent with similar monetary frameworks. The monetary policy frameworks are as follows.

Exchange rate anchor

The monetary authority buys or sells foreign exchange to maintain the exchange rate at its predetermined level or within a range. The exchange rate thus serves as the nominal anchor or intermediate target of monetary policy. These frameworks are associated with exchange rate arrangements with no separate legal tender, currency board arrangements, pegs

(or stabilized arrangements) with or without bands, crawling pegs (or crawl-like arrangements), and other managed arrangements.

Monetary aggregate target

The monetary authority uses its instruments to achieve a target growth rate for a monetary aggregate, such as reserve money, M1, or M2, and the targeted aggregate becomes the nominal anchor or intermediate target of monetary policy.

Inflation-targeting framework

This involves the public announcement of numerical targets for inflation, with an institutional commitment by the monetary authority to achieve these targets, typically over a medium-term horizon. Additional key features normally include increased communication with the public and the markets about the plans and objectives of monetary policymakers and increased accountability of the central bank for achieving its inflation objectives. Monetary policy decisions are often guided by the deviation of forecasts of future inflation from the announced inflation target, with the inflation forecast acting (implicitly or explicitly) as the intermediate target of monetary policy.

Other

The country has no explicitly stated nominal anchor, but rather monitors various indicators in conducting monetary policy. This category is also used when no relevant information on the country is available.

Table 1 (continued)

Exchange rate arrangement (number of countries)	Monetary Policy Framework						
	Exchange rate anchor				Monetary aggregate target (26)	Inflation-targeting framework (34)	Other[1] (39)
	U.S. dollar (44)	Euro (27)	Composite (13)	Other (8)			
No separate legal tender (13)	Ecuador El Salvador Marshall Islands Micronesia Palau Panama Timor-Leste Zimbabwe	Kosovo Montenegro San Marino		Kiribati Tuvalu			
Currency board (12)	**ECCU** Antigua and Barbuda Dominica Grenada St. Kitts and Nevis St. Lucia St. Vincent and the Grenadines Djibouti Hong Kong SAR	Bosnia and Herzegovina Bulgaria Lithuania[2]		Brunei Darussalam			
Conventional peg (45)	Aruba The Bahamas Bahrain Barbados Belize Curaçao and Sint Maarten Eritrea Jordan Oman Qatar Saudi Arabia Turkmenistan United Arab Emirates Venezuela	Cape Verde Comoros Denmark[2] Latvia[2] São Tomé and Príncipe **WAEMU** Benin Burkina Faso Côte d'Ivoire Guinea-Bissau Mali Niger Senegal Togo **CAEMC** Cameroon Central African Rep. Chad Congo, Rep. of Equatorial Guinea Gabon	Fiji Kuwait Libya Morocco[4] Samoa	Bhutan Lesotho Namibia Nepal Swaziland			Solomon Islands[5,6] (01/12)
Stabilized arrangement (19)	Cambodia Guyana Honduras Iraq Lebanon Maldives Suriname Trinidad and Tobago	Macedonia Vietnam[7]	Belarus (05/10) Iran Syria Tunisia		Congo, Dem. Rep. of the[5,7] (01/12) Tajikistan[7] Ukraine[7] Yemen[7] (06/12)	Georgia[7] (06/11)	Angola[7] Azerbaijan[7] Costa Rica[5,7] (04/12) Lao P.D.R.[7] Bolivia[5,7] (11/11)
Crawling peg (2)	Nicaragua		Botswana				
Crawl-like arrangement (15)	Ethiopia Honduras Jamaica Kazakhstan	Croatia	Singapore[5] (11/11)		Argentina[7] China[7] Rwanda[7] Uzbekistan[7]	Dominican Rep.[7] Indonesia[7] (06/12)	Egypt[5,7] (11/11) Haiti[7] Tunisia[6,8]
Pegged exchange rate within horizontal bands (1)			Tonga				
Other managed arrangement (19)	Liberia		Algeria Iran Syria Vanuatu		Bangladesh Burundi Guinea Kyrgyz Rep. Malawi Nigeria	Paraguay	Belarus Malaysia Mauritania Myanmar Russia[8] Sudan Switzerland[5,9] (01/13)

Table 1 (concluded)

Exchange rate arrangement (number of countries)	Monetary Policy Framework						
	Exchange rate anchor				Monetary aggregate target (26)	Inflation-targeting framework (34)	Other[1] (39)
	U.S. dollar (44)	Euro (27)	Composite (13)	Other (8)			

Floating (35)					Afghanistan
					The Gambia
					Kenya
					Madagascar
					Mozambique
					Papua New
					  Guinea[9]
					  (01/13)
					Seychelles
					Sierra Leone
					Sri Lanka
					  (02/12)
					Tanzania
					Uganda[8]
					Zambia
						Albania
						Armenia[6]
						Brazil
						Colombia
						Ghana
						Guatemala[5]
						  (03/12)
						Hungary
						Iceland
						Korea
						Mexico
						Moldova
						New Zea-
						  land
						  (11/12)
						Peru
						Philippines
						Romania
						Serbia
						South Africa
						Thailand
						Turkey
						Uruguay
							India
							Mauritius
							Mongolia
							Pakistan

Free floating (30)						Australia
						Canada
						Chile
						Czech Rep.
						Israel
						Japan
						Mexico
						Norway
						Poland
						Sweden
						United
						  Kingdom
							Somalia
							United
							  States
							
							EMU
							Austria
							Belgium
							Cyprus
							Estonia
							Finland
							France
							Germany
							Greece
							Ireland
							Italy
							Luxembourg
							Malta
							Netherlands
							Portugal
							Slovak Rep.
							Slovenia
							Spain

Source: IMF staff.

Note: If the member country's de facto exchange rate arrangement has been reclassified during the reporting period, the date of change is indicated in parentheses.

[1] Includes countries that have no explicitly stated nominal anchor but rather monitor various indicators in conducting monetary policy.

[2] The member participates in the European Exchange Rate Mechanism (ERM II).

[3] South Sudan became a member of the IMF on April 18, 2012. The de facto exchange rate arrangement classification was under review at the time the AREAER was finalized. Therefore, this table reflects the de jure exchange rate regime, which is a conventional peg vis-à-vis the U.S. dollar..

[4] Within the framework of an exchange rate fixed to a currency composite, the Bank Al-Maghrib adopted a monetary policy framework in 2006 based on various inflation indicators with the overnight interest rate as its operational target to pursue its main objective of price stability.

[5] The exchange rate arrangement was reclassified retroactively, overriding a previously published classification.

[6] The country maintains a de facto exchange rate anchor to a composite.

[7] The country maintains a de facto exchange rate anchor to the U.S. dollar.

[8] The central bank has taken preliminary steps toward inflation targeting.

[9] The exchange rate arrangement was reclassified twice during this reporting period, reverting to the classification in previous year's report.

- The number of countries with a conventional peg arrangement increased by 2, to 45. The Solomon Islands, which has a de jure conventional peg arrangement, stabilized the exchange rate and thus, after one year, its de facto exchange rate arrangement was reclassified back to a conventional peg. In addition, South Sudan adopted a de jure conventional peg exchange rate arrangement after introducing its own currency (and pegging it against the U.S. dollar) at the time of its independence in July 2011. Pending further review, South Sudan's de facto exchange rate arrangement is provisionally included in the conventional peg category.

- Although the number of stabilized arrangements increased only by 3—to 19—between April 30, 2012, and April 30, 2013, this category had the largest number of changes in the reporting period: 11 in all. Including temporary changes, seven countries entered and four countries left this group. Five new countries joined and remained in this group: Bolivia (previously crawling peg), Costa Rica (previously other managed arrangement), the Democratic Republic of the Congo (previously other managed arrangement), Georgia (previously floating), and Yemen (previously other managed arrangement). Two countries (Egypt and Guatemala) that left this group moved back to the exchange rate arrangement categories they had before the previous reporting period. Two other countries (Papua New Guinea and Switzerland) were classified as having stabilized arrangements for part of the reporting period but eventually reverted to their previous classifications.

- The number of countries with crawl-like arrangements increased from 12 to 15, with no countries leaving this group. The three countries that joined this group are Egypt (previously stabilized arrangement), Indonesia (previously floating), and Singapore (previously other managed arrangement).

- Tonga is the only country that maintains a pegged exchange rate within horizontal bands. Two additional countries have de jure pegged exchange rates within horizontal bands, but one of them has a de facto stabilized arrangement and the other has a de facto other managed arrangement.

- Five countries left the category other managed arrangement (the residual category); one country joined this group again after having been reclassified to another category for part of the reporting period (Switzerland, which was classified as having a stabilized arrangement for slightly over a year). Among the countries that left this group the majority moved to soft pegs. Three moved to stabilized arrangements (Democratic Republic of the Congo, Costa Rica, Yemen), one to a crawl-like arrangement (Singapore), and one to a conventional peg (Solomon Islands).

Table 2. Exchange Rate Arrangements, 2008–13

(Percent of IMF members as of April 30 each year)[1]

Exchange Rate Arrangements	2008[2]	2009[3]	2010[4]	2011[5]	2012[5]	2013
Hard pegs	12.2	12.2	13.2	13.2	13.2	13.1
No separate legal tender	5.3	5.3	6.3	6.8	6.8	6.8
Currency board	6.9	6.9	6.9	6.3	6.3	6.3
Soft pegs	39.9	34.6	39.7	43.2	39.5	42.9
Conventional peg	22.3	22.3	23.3	22.6	22.6	23.6
Stabilized arrangement	12.8	6.9	12.7	12.1	8.4	9.9
Crawling peg	2.7	2.7	1.6	1.6	1.6	1.0
Crawl-like arrangement	1.1	0.5	1.1	6.3	6.3	7.9
Pegged exchange rate within horizontal bands	1.1	2.1	1.1	0.5	0.5	0.5
Floating	39.9	42.0	36.0	34.7	34.7	34.0
Floating	20.2	24.5	20.1	18.9	18.4	18.3
Free floating	19.7	17.6	15.9	15.8	16.3	15.7
Residual						
Other managed arrangement	8.0	11.2	11.1	8.9	12.6	9.9

Source: AREAER database.

[1] Includes 188 member countries and three territories: Aruba (Netherlands), Curaçao and Sint Maarten (Netherlands), and Hong Kong SAR (China).

[2] As retroactively classified February 2, 2009; does not include Kosovo, Tuvalu, and South Sudan, which became IMF members on June 29, 2009, June 24, 2010, and April 18, 2012, respectively.

[3] As published in the 2009 AREAER; does not include Kosovo, Tuvalu, and South Sudan, which became IMF members on June 29, 2009, June 24, 2010, and April 18, 2012, respectively.

[4] As published in the 2010 AREAER; does not include Tuvalu and South Sudan, which became IMF members on June 24, 2010 and April 18, 2012, respectively.

[5] As published in the 2011 and 2012 AREAERs; does not include South Sudan, which became IMF member on April 18, 2012.

- The number of countries with floating arrangements remained stable (35), with several changes to the composition of the group. The same number of countries switched sides between the stabilized arrangement and floating categories: Georgia (previously floating) was reclassified to stabilized arrangement, and Guatemala (previously stabilized) was reclassified to floating; Papua New Guinea was classified as a stabilized arrangement for part of the period before returning to floating. Indonesia left this group to be reclassified as having a crawl-like arrangement, but this was offset by the addition of New Zealand, previously in the free-floating category.

- The number of countries classified as having free-floating arrangements declined by 1, to 30. New Zealand was reclassified as floating after the volume of the Reserve Bank of New Zealand's net New Zealand dollar sales started to increase in November 2012.

Table 3. Changes and Resulting Reclassifications of Exchange Rate Arrangements, January 1, 2012–April 30, 2013

Country	Change	Previous Arrangement[1]	Arrangement in the 2013 AREAER
Bolivia[2]	Within the scope of the official crawling peg exchange rate regime, in an external environment of marked exchange rate volatility and decreasing external inflation, the sliding rate was set at zero. Consequently, the boliviano stabilized anew against the U.S. dollar since November 2011. Accordingly, the de facto exchange rate arrangement was retroactively reclassified to a stabilized arrangement from a crawling peg, effective November 2, 2011. However, the change is reflected as of January 1, 2012, corresponding to the first day of the period covered in this year's AREAER.	Crawling peg	Stabilized arrangement
Costa Rica[2]	Since mid-April 2012, the colon–U.S. dollar exchange rate remained within a 2% band vis-à-vis the lower bound of the exchange rate band and was occasionally at the lower bound level itself, prompting the Central Bank of Costa Rica to intervene to prevent the colon from appreciating further. Given the stability of the exchange rate, the de facto exchange rate arrangement was retroactively reclassified to a stabilized arrangement from other managed arrangement, effective April 16, 2012.	Other managed arrangement	Stabilized arrangement
Democratic Republic of the Congo[2]	After departing from the stabilized band in November 2011 with increased flexibility for several months, the Congo franc stabilized anew against the U.S. dollar in early January 2012. Accordingly, the de facto exchange rate arrangement was retroactively reclassified to a stabilized arrangement from other managed, effective January 1, 2012.	Other managed arrangement	Stabilized arrangement
Egypt[2]	Following a period of stability against the U.S. dollar, the pound, in mid-November 2011, started on a depreciating trend against the dollar within a margin of less than 2% with a one-time adjustment in January 2013. Accordingly, the de facto exchange rate arrangement was retroactively reclassified to a crawl-like arrangement from a stabilized arrangement, effective November 10, 2011. This change is reflected as of January 1, 2012, corresponding to the first day of the period covered in this year's AREAER.	Stabilized arrangement	Crawl-like arrangement
Georgia	Since July 2012, the lari has remained stable against the U.S. dollar in a 2% band. Market supply and demand play a role in determining the exchange rate, as does official action based on the observed path of the exchange rate and the discretionary nature of the foreign exchange auctions. Therefore, the de facto exchange rate arrangement was reclassified from floating to a stabilized arrangement against the U.S. dollar, effective July 1, 2012.	Floating	Stabilized arrangement

Table 3 (continued)

Country	Change	Previous Arrangement[1]	Arrangement in the 2013 AREAER
Guatemala[2]	After a period of relative stability from June 2011 through early March 2012, the quetzal showed increased flexibility against the U.S. dollar without an ascertainable path for the exchange rate. Accordingly, the de facto exchange rate arrangement was retroactively reclassified to floating from a stabilized arrangement, effective March 13, 2012.	Stabilized arrangement	Floating
Indonesia	Since June 2012, the rupiah followed a depreciating trend against the U.S. dollar within a margin of less than 2%. Accordingly, the de facto exchange rate arrangement was reclassified to crawl-like arrangement from floating, effective June 1, 2012.	Floating	Crawl-like arrangement
New Zealand	There was an increase in the volume of net New Zealand dollars sold by the Reserve Bank of New Zealand since November 2012, continuing through April 2013. Accordingly, the de facto exchange rate arrangement was reclassified to floating from free floating, effective November 1, 2012.	Free floating	Floating
Papua New Guinea[2]	From mid-February 2012 through the end of December 2012, the kina remained stable against the U.S. dollar within a 2% band. Accordingly, the de facto exchange rate arrangement was retroactively reclassified to a stabilized arrangement from floating, effective February 23, 2012.	Floating	Stabilized arrangement
Papua New Guinea[3]	In January 2013, the exchange rate departed from the stabilized band and has shown increased flexibility since. Therefore, the de facto exchange rate arrangement was reclassified to floating from a stabilized arrangement, effective January 1, 2013.		Floating
Singapore[2]	After falling to the lower half of the policy band in September and October 2011, the Singapore dollar resumed its previous course and followed an appreciating trend against a basket of currencies within a 2% band since November 2011. Therefore, the de facto exchange rate arrangement was retroactively reclassified to a crawl-like arrangement from other managed, effective November 9, 2011. The change is reflected as of January 1, 2012, corresponding to the first day of the period covered in this year's AREAER.	Other managed arrangement	Crawl-like arrangement
Solomon Islands[2]	After a period of gradual appreciation against the U.S. dollar, the Solomon Islands dollar has been stable against the dollar within a 2% band since January 30, 2012. Therefore, the de facto exchange rate arrangement was retroactively reclassified to a conventional peg from other managed arrangement, effective January 30, 2012.	Other managed arrangement	Conventional peg
Sri Lanka	Following a period of stability in the exchange rate, the authorities limited their intervention in the foreign exchange market and allowed increased flexibility against the U.S. dollar. As a result, the rupee–U.S. dollar exchange rate departed from the stabilized band and moved more freely. Accordingly, the de facto exchange rate arrangement was reclassified to floating from a stabilized arrangement, effective February 9, 2012.	Stabilized arrangement	Floating
Switzerland[2]	From January 2012 through mid-January 2013, the Swiss franc remained within a narrower 2% margin of the announced minimum exchange rate. Therefore, the de facto exchange rate arrangement was retroactively reclassified to a stabilized arrangement from other managed arrangement, effective January 1, 2012.	Other managed arrangement	Stabilized arrangement

Table 3 (concluded)

Country	Change	Previous Arrangement[1]	Arrangement in the 2013 AREAER
Switzerland[3]	Following a period of stability, around mid-January 2013, the franc departed from the stabilized band against the euro with limited flexibility, while the authorities' commitment to defending the minimum exchange rate remained unchanged. Accordingly, the de facto exchange rate arrangement was reclassified to other managed arrangement from a stabilized arrangement, effective January 14, 2013.		Other managed arrangement
Yemen	Due to the unification of the official and parallel market rates and stability of the exchange rate against the U.S. dollar since June 2012, the de facto exchange rate arrangement was reclassified to a stabilized arrangement from other managed arrangement, effective June 1, 2012.	Other managed arrangement	Stabilized arrangement

Source: AREAER database.

[1] This column refers to the arrangements as reported in the 2012 AREAER, except in cases when a reclassification took place during January 1–April 30, 2012, in which case it refers to the arrangement preceding such a reclassification.

[2] The exchange rate arrangement was reclassified retroactively, overriding a previously published classification for the entire reporting period or part of the period.

[3] Cells in the column "Previous Arrangement" are blank if there was a subsequent reclassification during the reporting period.

Monetary Anchors[9]

The exchange rate remained the anchor for monetary policy for fewer than half of member countries (Table 4). This reporting period has been remarkably quiet in terms of developments in official monetary anchors,[10] following two years of significant recategorization, in part because of improved reporting.[11] Among exchange rate anchors, the only change reflects the addition of South Sudan with a peg against the U.S. dollar. There were a few more changes among the other categories. Overall, with four switches between the categories and one new member joining with a U.S. dollar anchor, the number of members using the U.S. dollar as a monetary anchor (44) increased slightly, whereas the number of members using the euro (27), a composite (13), or another single currency (8) remained the same (see Table 1).

Fifty-seven member countries have an officially announced fixed exchange rate policy—either a currency board or a conventional peg—which implies the use of the exchange rate as the unique monetary anchor, with one exception. Although the official (de jure) exchange rate regime of the Solomon Islands is a peg against a basket of currencies (effective October 1, 2012), the monetary policy framework was reported to comprise a mix of anchors, including the exchange rate. Among the 65 countries that have floating exchange rate arrangements—floating or free floating—the monetary anchor does not refer to the exchange rate and varies among monetary aggregates (12), inflation targeting (30), and other (23, including the 17 euro area countries). Fourteen countries implementing soft pegs and other managed arrangements target monetary aggregates. Countries with either stabilized or crawl-like arrangements (34) rely on a variety of monetary frameworks, including monetary aggregates and inflation-targeting frameworks. Paraguay is the only country classified as other managed arrangement with an inflation-targeting framework; the remaining other managed arrangements are almost equally split between monetary aggregate targets (6) and other monetary policy frameworks (7).

---

[9] Monetary anchors are defined as the main intermediate target the authorities pursue to achieve their policy goal (which is overwhelmingly price stability). The inventory of monetary anchors is based mainly on members' declaration in the context of the yearly AREAER update or Article IV consultations.

[10] The officially announced monetary anchor may differ from the anchor implemented in practice, as a result of the de facto exchange rate arrangement.

[11] For the 2010 reporting year, country officials were asked for the first time to report specific information about the monetary policy framework, and as a result, the information provided by officials improved considerably.

Table 4. Monetary Policy Frameworks and Exchange Rate Anchors

(Percent of IMF members as of April 30 each year)[1]

	U.S. Dollar	Euro	Composite	Other Currency	Monetary Aggregate	Inflation Targeting	Other[2]
2008[3]	33.0	14.4	8.0	3.7	11.7	22.9	6.4
2009[3]	28.7	14.4	7.4	4.3	13.3	15.4	16.5
2010[4]	26.5	14.8	7.9	3.7	13.2	16.4	17.5
2011[5]	25.3	14.2	7.4	4.2	15.3	16.3	17.4
2012[5]	22.6	14.2	6.8	4.2	15.3	16.8	20.0
2013	23.0	14.1	6.8	4.2	13.6	17.8	20.4

Source: AREAER database.

Note: When the de facto exchange rate arrangement differs from the de jure arrangement, the monetary anchor indicated in this table reflects the de facto arrangement.

[1] Includes 188 member countries and three territories: Aruba, Curaçao and Sint Maarten (all Netherlands) and Hong Kong SAR (China).

[2] Includes countries that have no explicitly stated nominal anchor but instead monitor various indicators in conducting monetary policy. This category is also used when no relevant information on the country is available.

[3] Does not include Kosovo, Tuvalu, and South Sudan, which became IMF members on June 29, 2009, June 24, 2010, and April 18, 2012, respectively.

[4] Does not include Tuvalu and South Sudan, which became IMF members on June 24, 2010, and April 18, 2012, respectively.

[5] Does not include South Sudan, which became an IMF member on April 18, 2012.

- The share of IMF members with the exchange rate as the main policy target increased only slightly, from 47.9 percent to 48.2 percent. This increase is due solely to the new member, South Sudan. Countries with hard pegs or conventional pegs make up three-quarters of this group. Three currency unions—the Central African Economic and Monetary Community (CAEMC), Eastern Caribbean Currency Union (ECCU), and Western African Economic and Monetary Union (WAEMU)—have exchange rate anchors for their respective common currency. However, these countries account for less than 20 percent of global output and world trade. Exchange rate anchors are by far the first choice of small, open economies, as suggested in the economic literature.

- The U.S. dollar maintained its position as the dominant exchange rate anchor, having increased slightly with the addition of South Sudan after five years of consistent contraction since April 2008. Countries that continue to anchor to the dollar also include those with moderate trade relations with the United States.

- There was no change in the share or composition of countries using an exchange rate anchor to the euro. These countries, such as the Communauté financière d'Afrique (CFA) franc area countries, generally have a common history with European countries or strong trade relations with western Europe, including central and eastern European countries such as Bulgaria, the former Yugoslav Republic of Macedonia, Montenegro, and San Marino.

- Thirteen countries anchor their exchange rate to a currency composite. Four track the SDR as the sole currency basket or as a component of a broader reference basket; one tracks a euro–U.S. dollar basket; two Pacific island countries track a composite that includes the Australian and New Zealand dollars in combination with major global currencies; and the remaining six countries do not disclose the composition of their reference currency baskets.

- The number of countries with an exchange rate anchor to another single currency remained unchanged (8). Two of these countries use the Australian dollar as their legal currency, and one has a currency board arrangement with the Singapore dollar. The remaining five have conventional pegged arrangements, three with the South African rand and two with the Indian rupee. Half the countries in this group are landlocked, bordering either partially or exclusively the country whose currency they use as their exchange rate anchor

Most IMF member countries, representing the overwhelming share of global output, are split among monetary aggregate targeting, inflation targeting, and other (which includes monetary policy not committed to any specific target).

- The number of countries targeting a monetary aggregate declined from 29 in April 2012 to 26 in April 2013.[12] This category does not include any country with a free-floating exchange rate arrangement; in fact, monetary aggregates are often the choice of economies with less-developed financial markets and managed exchange rates. The objective of the arrangement is to influence consumer prices and eventually asset prices through the control of monetary aggregates. Reserve money is often used as the operational target to control credit growth through the credit multiplier. During the past year, two countries switched from monetary aggregate targeting to other monetary framework (Mongolia and Pakistan), and one country switched to inflation targeting (Paraguay).

- The number of countries that directly target inflation increased by two (Japan and Paraguay).[13] After the initial introduction of a price stability goal in 2012, Japan implemented the price stability target under the monetary policy framework and set the target at 2 percent in January 2013. These significant developments underline that an inflation-targeting framework is increasingly the choice among advanced economies and not only middle-income economies. Of the inflation-targeting countries, 30 have either floating or free-floating exchange rate arrangements, a policy framework that requires considerable monetary authority credibility to make up for the loss of transparent intermediate targets.[14] A few countries refer to their monetary framework as "inflation targeting light," suggesting that they also consider indicators other than inflation. During the past year, one other country, Paraguay, joined this group by adopting inflation targeting as its formal monetary policy after completing the transition stage. Furthermore, Russia and Uganda are in the transition stage to full-fledged inflation targeting.[15]

- The number of countries that are not committed to any specific target (the "other" column in Table 1) increased by 1 to 39. Mongolia and Pakistan now report a multiple indicator approach to monetary policy, while Japan formally adopted an inflation-targeting framework. This category includes many of the largest economies, such as the euro area and the United States, where the monetary authorities have sufficient credibility to implement the monetary framework without a specific monetary anchor. Countries in this category also include those with multiple monetary anchors, often including an exchange rate anchor. For example, Pakistan, which previously targeted only monetary aggregates, was reclassified to "other" monetary policy framework because it now seeks to control inflation in the policy mix. Similarly, Mongolia reports monitoring a broad range of financial and real indicators in the conduct of monetary policy.

Foreign Exchange Interventions

The IMF staff regularly assesses whether the frequency of foreign exchange intervention is consistent with de facto free-floating arrangements (see the Compilation Guide).[16] These assessments draw on information that is publicly available and made available to the IMF through other sources, including during official staff visits to member countries. This section summarizes developments in foreign exchange interventions since January 1, 2012, some of which are also depicted in Table 5 and Table 7.a.

---

[12] As of July 1, 2013, Uruguay replaced the overnight interest rate as its operational target with a monetary aggregate target (M1 plus savings deposits).

[13] Although the United States did not switch to an inflation-targeting framework, the Federal Open Market Committee announced inflation at the rate of 2 percent to be most consistent with the Federal Reserve's statutory mandate.

[14] Inflation targeting aims to address the problem of exchange rates and monetary aggregates that do not have a stable relationship with prices, making intermediary targets less suitable for inflation control.

[15] The Central Bank of the Russian Federation (Bank of Russia) has taken preliminary steps toward a free-floating exchange rate regime.

[16] Preannounced programs of purchases and/or sales of foreign exchange typically do not qualify as interventions because the design of these programs minimizes the impact on the exchange rate. Very small, retail-type transactions are also disregarded.

Intervention Purpose

The developments related to official interventions paint a mixed picture. There has been no reported intervention in major advanced economies (for example, Japan, euro area). However, against the backdrop of increased capital flow volatility, there has been mounting pressure on smaller advanced economies and emerging market economies. The heightened intervention activity was evident in self-reporting, various market reports, and significant changes in some members' foreign exchange reserves.

After intervening several times in 2011, Japan ceased its official foreign exchange activities in 2012 and early 2013. On the other hand, New Zealand responded to heavy appreciation pressure by increasing its foreign exchange purchases. The Czech Republic announced additional monetary easing in the form of foreign exchange interventions while suspending sales of foreign exchange reserve revenues.

In some countries, exchange rate pressure reflects domestic conditions rather than the global environment. Faced with significant volatility against the backdrop of political protests, Turkey resumed (see Table 7.a) its intraday foreign exchange selling auctions in June 2013 after suspending the regular selling auctions in January 2012 and the intraday auctions in January 2013. Leaning the other way, Israel announced, in May 2013, a foreign exchange purchase plan (see Table 5) to offset the effect of natural gas production on the exchange rate, estimating total purchases to be about US$2.1 billion by the end of 2013 within the framework of this plan.

Intervention Techniques

In 2012, to combat massive overvaluation and defend the minimum exchange rate, the Swiss National Bank increased its purchases to approximately Sw F 188 billion in foreign currency (compared with Sw F 17.8 billion in 2011) with a wide range of counterparties in Switzerland and abroad.

Turkey's central bank introduced the reserve option mechanism (ROM) as a new monetary policy tool, while gradually phasing out its foreign exchange auctions. In this framework, the central bank grants banks the option to hold a fraction of their mandatory reserves for Turkish lira liabilities in foreign currency and gold. The ROM, which largely replaced the role of auctions and bilateral interventions, has been used as an active policy tool by the central bank and may have contributed to stabilizing capital flow volatility, indirectly influencing exchange rate movements. However, Turkey had to resort to a large volume of foreign exchange auctions when faced with significant volatility in June 2013.

Russia continued to ease the rules guiding its interventions by further widening the band (from Rub 6 to Rub 7) for allowable fluctuations and reducing the cumulative amount of unplanned interventions triggering an automatic adjustment of the exchange rate band by 5 kopeks (US$500 million to US$450 million). Furthermore, foreign exchange interventions are now reported with a two-day lag (previously, one-week lag). Similarly, Guatemala widened the fluctuation margin triggering interventions from 0.6 percent to 0.65 percent.

Table 5. Changes in Exchange Rate Arrangements, Official Exchange Rate, and Monetary Policy Framework, January 1, 2012–August 31, 2013

Country	Change
Albania	Effective January 16, 2012, the Bank of Albania (BOA) adopted a policy to accumulate an adequate level of foreign reserves in the medium term that would cover more than four months of imports and the short-term external debt of the country. Previously, the BOA intervened in order to meet the net international reserves target, which was included each year in its monetary program.
Burundi	Effective March 12, 2012, the Bank of the Republic of Burundi began determining the reference rate each morning on the basis of the weighted average of commercial banks' foreign exchange buying and selling transactions with their customers on the previous day, excluding transactions through the Marché des Enchères Symétriques en Devises (MESD). Previously, the rate was based on its MESD auctions.
Burundi	Effective April 12, 2013, with the replacement of the Marché des Enchères Symétriques en Devises with the Marché Interbancaire des Devises, the method for calculating the reference rate was modified to include all Bank of the Republic of Burundi (BRB) transactions with its customers on the previous day. To prevent a recurrence of sharp fluctuations, bank operations for which the exchange rate deviates from the defined band are systematically excluded from the calculations. Previously, the BRB determined the reference rate each morning based on the weighted average of commercial banks' foreign exchange buying and selling transactions with their customers on the previous day, excluding BRB transactions through the Marché des Enchères Symétriques en Devises.
Costa Rica	Effective January 25, 2012, in order to reinforce the economy's "financial shield," the board of directors of the Central Bank of Costa Rica, in Article 7 of Meeting 5532-2012 of January 25, 2012, agreed to implement a new program to build international reserves between February 1, 2012, and December 31, 2013, up to US$1,500 million.
Czech Republic	Effective September 27, 2012, the Czech National Bank (CNB) announced additional monetary easing within the context of the inflation-targeting framework from foreign exchange interventions given that the interest rate reached the zero lower bound. As of April 30, 2013, the CNB has not used this foreign exchange intervention tool.
Czech Republic	Effective November 1, 2012, the Czech National Bank suspended sales of foreign exchange reserve revenues, which were aimed at preventing a continued rise in the reserve level, and began to publish monthly foreign exchange transaction data on its website, with a two-month lag.
Dominican Republic	Effective January 1, 2012, pursuant to a resolution on December 15, 2011, of the Monetary Board, the Central Bank of the Dominican Republic adopted explicit inflation targeting as its monetary policy framework.
Egypt	Effective July 10, 2012, in addition to the 7-day repurchase agreements introduced in March 2011, 28-day repurchase agreements (introduced June 14, 2012, by the Central Bank of Egypt) became part of Egypt's monetary policy framework.
Guatemala	Effective January 1, 2012, the annual inflation target was set at 4.5% ±1% for 2012.
Guatemala	Effective January 1, 2013, the annual inflation target was set at 4.0% ±1% for 2013.
Iraq	Effective January 17, 2012, the Central Bank of Iraq reduced the level around which it stabilizes the exchange rate from ID 1,170 to ID 1,166 per U.S. dollar.
Iraq	Effective April 15, 2013, the Central Bank of Iraq sells foreign exchange to banks for import letters of credit by adding ID 9 per U.S. dollar to the auction exchange rate. For other import transactions the Central Bank of Iraq adds ID 13 per U.S. dollar.
Israel	Effective May 13, 2013, the Bank of Israel (BOI) announced a foreign exchange purchase plan to offset the effect of natural gas production on the exchange rate, estimating the total purchases to be about $2.1 billion by the end of 2013 within the framework of this plan. The BOI's assessments of the overall effect on the balance of payments resulting from natural gas production and foreign exchange purchases will be updated from time to time and publicized. In line with this framework, prior to the May 13 announcement, the BOI had intervened in the foreign exchange market, albeit not more than three times through the end of April.
Japan	Effective February 14, 2012, the Bank of Japan (BOJ) introduced the "price stability goal in the medium to long term" as a part of its efforts to further clarify the determination to overcome deflation and achieve sustainable growth with price stability. The price stability goal is the inflation rate the BOJ considers consistent with price stability sustainable in the medium to long term. The BOJ considers "the price stability goal in the medium to long term" to be in a positive range of 2% or lower in terms of the year-over-year rate of change in the consumer price index and, more specifically, set a goal of 1% at the time of this announcement. Before introduction of this goal, the "understanding of medium- to long-term price stability" showed a range of inflation rates that each Policy Board member understood as price stability from a medium- to long-term perspective.

Table 5 (continued)

Country	Change
Japan	Effective January 22, 2013, the Bank of Japan (BOJ) introduced the "price stability target" under the framework for the conduct of monetary policy. Replacing a "goal" with a "target" and setting that target at 2% in terms of the year-over-year rate of change in the consumer price index are based on the following: (1) Because prices are expected to rise moderately, it is judged appropriate to clearly indicate the target of 2% in order to anchor the sustainable rate of inflation. (2) Switching from a "goal" to a "target" reflects increasing awareness of the importance of flexibility in the conduct of monetary policy in Japan. Recognizing that the inflation rate consistent with price stability on a sustainable basis will rise as efforts by a wide range of entities toward strengthening Japan's competitiveness and growth potential progress, the BOJ has set the target at 2% for year-over-year change in the consumer price index.
Japan	Effective April 4, 2013, the BOJ introduced "quantitative and qualitative monetary easing", maintaining the target of 2% in terms of the year-on-year rate of change in the consumer price index (CPI), with a time horizon of about two years. Under the new monetary policy framework, it will double the monetary base and the amounts outstanding of Japanese government bonds (JGBs) as well as exchange-traded funds (ETFs) in two years, and more than double the average remaining maturity of JGB purchases.
Korea	Effective January 1, 2013, the inflation target for 2013 onward is 2.5–3.5% based on the year-over-year average change in the consumer price index. The target horizon is three years (2013–15).
Malawi	Effective May 7, 2012, in anticipation of devaluation, the Reserve Bank of Malawi took steps aimed at allowing market forces to determine the exchange rate and at improved availability of foreign exchange in the market. Accordingly, the Reserve Bank of Malawi implemented the revised Guidelines for Foreign Exchange Trading Activities, allowing more market determination of the exchange rate.
Malawi	Effective May 7, 2012, the Reserve Bank of Malawi devalued the kwacha from MK 168 to MK 250 per U.S. dollar.
Morocco	Effective March 27, 2012, the Bank Al-Maghrib reference interest rate was reduced to 3.0% from 3.25%.
Myanmar	Effective April 2, 2012, the de jure exchange rate arrangement was reclassified to a managed float from a conventional peg to the SDR at K 8.50847 per SDR.
Myanmar	Effective April 2, 2012, the cutoff rate in the daily foreign exchange auction held by the Central Bank of Myanmar is used as the reference exchange rate for that day's trading. Previously, the kyat was officially pegged to the SDR at K 8.50847 per SDR within a margin of ±2%.
New Zealand	Based on a speech delivered by the Reserve Bank of New Zealand (RBNZ) governor on May 30, 2013, the RBNZ undertook foreign exchange transactions to dampen some of the spikes in the exchange rate in the earlier months, and the RBNZ is prepared to scale up foreign exchange activities if there are opportunities to have greater influence on the exchange rate.
Russia	Effective May 1, 2012, the Bank of Russia (BR) began reporting daily foreign exchange intervention data with a two-day lag, with historical data back to January 1, 2011. Previously, since June 2011, the BR published weekly foreign exchange intervention data with a one-week lag.
Russia	Effective July 24, 2012, the Bank of Russia widened the band of allowable fluctuation of the ruble from Rub 6 to Rub 7 and reduced the cumulative amount of unplanned interventions triggering an automatic adjustment of the exchange rate band by 5 kopeks from US$500 million to US$450 million.
San Marino	Effective September 1, 2012, a new monetary agreement between San Marino and the European Union, signed March 27, 2012, went into effect, repealing the previous agreement of November 29, 2000. The new agreement authorizes San Marino to use the euro as its official currency, grant legal tender status to euro banknotes and coins, and issue limited quantities of euro coins (as did the former agreement). Under the new agreement, San Marino commits to adopting relevant EU legislation regarding (1) money laundering, (2) fraud and forgery, (3) euro banknotes and coins, (4) banking and financial legislation, and (5) rules on the collection of statistical data within the time specified by the agreement (1–6 years) from implementation of the agreement (on euro banknotes and coins; combating fraud and counterfeiting; banking and financial legislation, including the prevention of money laundering and statistical reporting requirements) within the time specified by that agreement (1–6 years from the date of entry into effect—Decree No. 120 of August 7, 2012).
Serbia	Effective July 18, 2012, the National Bank of Serbia changed its main open market operations from two-week reverse repo transactions (liquidity absorbing) to one-week repo transactions (liquidity providing).

Table 5 (concluded)

Country	Change
Serbia	Effective September 9, 2012, the Russian ruble has been added to the list of currencies (previously, 16 currencies, now 17 including the Russian ruble) against which the official middle exchange rates of the dinar are quoted in the National Bank of Serbia list of official exchange rates and are used for bookkeeping, statistics, and calculation of customs duty and other import fees, as provided by Article 41 of the Foreign Exchange Law. Also, the list of foreign currencies and cash that banks may trade and of foreign cash that licensed exchange dealers may buy and sell was expanded to include Russian rubles (Decision on the Types of Foreign Exchange and Foreign Cash to Be Purchased and Sold in the Foreign Exchange Market—RS Official Gazette No. 98/2012).
Serbia	Effective December 19, 2012, the National Bank of Serbia changed its main open market operations from one-week repo transactions (liquidity providing) to one-week reverse repo transactions (liquidity absorbing).
Solomon Islands	Effective October 1, 2012, the de jure exchange rate regime is classified as a peg against a basket of currencies. Previously, the exchange rate policy of the Central Bank of the Solomon Islands (CBSI) was a peg against the U.S. dollar. The change in policy is based on price stability through greater flexibility to absorb global commodity price movements. However, to prevent large fluctuations in the rate and protect exporters and gross foreign reserves from undue volatility, the CBSI capped exchange rate movement to ±1% around the base rate. The new basket gives the greatest weight to the U.S. dollar, which accounts for 58% of total weight. The Australian dollar is the second largest at 32%. The remaining currencies are the New Zealand dollar at 5%, the yen at 3%, and the pound sterling at 2%.
Solomon Islands	Effective January 1, 2013, the new Central Bank Act—CBSI Act 2012—passed by the Parliament in November 2012 went into effect. Section 16 states that without limiting the primary objective of domestic price stability, (1) the government may after consultation with the Central Bank of the Solomon Islands (CBSI) determine the exchange rate regime; and (2) the CBSI may, after consultation with the minister of finance, determine and implement the exchange rate policy and enter into foreign exchange arrangements.
Solomon Islands	Effective April 17, 2013, the Central Bank of the Solomon Islands (CBSI) conducted a survey on exchange rate developments and administration since 2000. It sent an exchange rate questionnaire to banks, private companies, exporters, importers, and other stakeholders. The objective of the survey was to assess whether the CBSI should consider further revision of the exchange rate administration.
Tunisia	Effective April 18, 2012, a fixing arrangement (i.e., the average of market participants' quotes) replaced the currency composite as the reference exchange rate published by the Central Bank of Tunisia.
United States	Effective January 25, 2012, the Federal Open Market Committee (FOMC) announced that inflation at the rate of 2%, as measured by the annual change in the price index for personal consumption expenditures, was most consistent over the longer term with the Federal Reserve's statutory mandate. In setting monetary policy, the FOMC will seek to mitigate deviations in inflation from its longer-term goal and deviations in employment from the FOMC's assessment of its maximum level.
Zambia	Effective April 2, 2012, in preparation for a transition from targeting reserve money to targeting the interest rate by means of a key policy interest rate, the Bank of Zambia (BOZ) introduced the BOZ policy rate as another anchor of monetary policy.

Source: AREAER database

Official Exchange Rates

The vast majority (168) of IMF member countries report publishing official exchange rates. This includes not only countries that have officially determined and/or enforced exchange rates; by definition it also refers to any reference or indicative exchange rate that is computed and/or published by the central bank. The calculation of such exchange rates is often based on market exchange rates, such as exchange rates used in interbank market transactions or in a combination of interbank and bank-client transactions in a specified observation period. The published exchange rate is used as a guidance for market participants or for accounting and customs valuation purposes, in exchange transactions with the government, and sometimes mandatorily in specific exchange transactions. One new member, South Sudan, alongside El Salvador and Kenya, joined this group during the 2012–13 reporting period, while Japan reported no reference exchange rate published by the Bank of Japan. Among the 22 members that report no official or reference exchange rates, more than half (12) are countries with no separate legal tender.

Foreign Exchange Markets

Between January 1, 2012, and August 31, 2013, there were only minor changes in the reported foreign exchange market structure of members (Table 6). The most noteworthy developments were the increase in the number of countries with foreign exchange mechanisms operated by the central bank (by 3) and in the number of countries that have over-the-counter interbank markets (by 7). Table 7.a. includes detailed descriptions of changes concerning foreign exchange market arrangements.

Table 6. Foreign Exchange Market Structure, 2009–13

(Number of IMF members as of April 30 each year)[1]

	2009[2]	2010[3]	2011	2012	2013
Spot exchange market	**179**	**183**	**186**	**187**	**188**
Operated by the central bank	84	105	117	115	118
Foreign exchange standing facility	. . .	. . .	80	77	76
Allocation	29	29	31	30	31
Auction	31	29	26	29	31
Fixing	8	5	5	5	5
Interbank market	137	151	157	159	161
Over the counter	. . .	. . .	109	115	122
Brokerage	. . .	. . .	45	46	49
Market making	. . .	. . .	73	71	73
Forward exchange market	**127**	**126**	**128**	**127**	**129**

Source: AREAER database.
Note: . . . indicates that information on the arrangement was not separately collected during this period.
[1] Includes 188 member countries and three territories: Aruba (Netherlands), Curaçao and Sint Maarten (Netherlands), and Hong Kong SAR (China).
[2] Does not include Kosovo, Tuvalu, and South Sudan, which became IMF members on June 29, 2009, June 24, 2010, and April 18, 2012, respectively.
[3] Does not include Tuvalu and South Sudan, which became IMF members on June 24, 2010, and April 18, 2012, respectively.
[4] Does not include South Sudan, which became an IMF member on April 18, 2012.

Table 7.a. Changes in Foreign Exchange Markets, January 1, 2012–August 31, 2013

Country	Change	Type
Afghanistan	Effective November 17, 2012, the settlement period for Da Afghanistan Bank's foreign currency auctions was shortened to within the same day from two days.	Tightening
Afghanistan	Effective March 6, 2013, the settlement period for Da Afghanistan Bank's foreign currency auctions was changed to T + 1 from within the same day.	Easing
Afghanistan	Effective March 18, 2013, the fine for successful bidders who fail to settle their account within T + 1 days was raised to US$20,000 from US$10,000.	Tightening
Bolivia	Effective January 2, 2012, the fee on outward funds transfers by the financial system through the Central Bank of Bolivia was set at 1%, and the fee on inward funds transfers by the financial system through the Central Bank of Bolivia was set at 0.6%.	Tightening
Bolivia	Effective July 24, 2012, the financial transaction tax was extended for 36 months from the effective date by Law No. 234 of April 13, 2012.	Tightening
Bolivia	Effective October 12, 2012, the Central Bank of Bolivia began to offer US$150 million daily. The demand for foreign exchange has not exceeded this amount.	Neutral

Table 7.a (continued)

Country	Change	Type
Burundi	Effective March 12, 2012, the Bank of the Republic of Burundi (BRB) made the following changes to the Marché des Enchères Symétriques en Devises: (1) The frequency of auctions was lowered from five to two a week, on Tuesdays and Thursdays at 9:30 a.m. (2) Foreign currencies was allocated at the offered rates (multiple rates) instead of the single marginal rate. (3) In order to promote the interbank market, banks could not purchase foreign exchange from or sell it to the BRB outside of the market.	Tightening
Burundi	Effective March 1, 2013, in support of measures to set the fluctuation band for the foreign exchange rate and arrest depreciation of the franc, the Bank of the Republic of Burundi increased its intervention in the Marché des Enchères Symétriques en Devises by selling US$8,958,098.88 in accordance with the new intervention procedures. The weighted average rate resulting from this intervention (FBu–US$1,569.2) was adopted as the reference rate for the next business day, i.e., March 4, 2013, which reversed the trend toward depreciation and brought the rate from FBu 1,724.27 on March 1 to FBu–US$1,569.2 on March 4, 2013.	Tightening
Burundi	Effective March 1, 2013, the Bank of the Republic of Burundi set a fluctuation margin on foreign currency buying and selling transactions by commercial banks and exchange bureaus of ±1% of the reference rate it publishes each morning.	Tightening
Burundi	Effective April 12, 2013, the Bank of the Republic of Burundi (BRB) discontinued the Marché des Enchères Symétriques en Devises (MESD), which had lost its symmetry. Only the BRB was intervening in the MESD despite the assumption that it was driven by commercial banks, with the BRB intervening only as a last resort.	Easing
Burundi	Effective April 12, 2013, the Bank of the Republic of Burundi (BRB) established an interbank foreign exchange market, the Marché Interbancaire des Devises, to replace the Marché des Enchères Symétriques en Devises, which had lost its symmetry. To encourage banks to trade currencies and promote the interbank market, the BRB acted to prevent exchange bureaus from procuring foreign exchange from commercial banks. The new regulations governing the interbank foreign exchange market allow the BRB to intervene on its own initiative in accordance with market conditions.	Easing
China	Effective April 16, 2012, the floating band of the RMB's trading prices against the U.S. dollar in the interbank foreign exchange market was widened from 0.5% to 1%—i.e., on each business day, the trading prices of the RMB against the U.S. dollar in the interbank foreign exchange market may fluctuate within a band of ±1% around the central parity released on the same day by the China Foreign Exchange Trade System. The spread between the highest offer price and the lowest bid price of RMB–U.S. dollar spot transactions, as quoted by foreign-exchange-designated banks to their customers, may not exceed 2% of the central parity (previously 1%).	Easing
Colombia	Effective February 6, 2012, the Bank of the Republic suspended the options auction mechanism and resumed daily foreign exchange purchases of at least US$20 million to increase the level of international reserves through competitive auctions for at least three consecutive months.	Neutral
Colombia	Effective February 24, 2012, the Bank of the Republic extended the program of daily purchases of a minimum of US$20 million to at least August 4, 2012.	Neutral
Colombia	Effective April 30, 2012, the Bank of the Republic extended the program of daily purchases of a minimum of US$20 million to at least November 2, 2012.	Neutral
Colombia	Effective August 24, 2012, a total purchase amount of US$700 million through daily auctions for the remainder of August and September was announced.	Neutral
Colombia	Effective September 28, 2012, the Bank of the Republic extended the program of daily purchases of a minimum of US$20 million to at least March 30, 2013, with a total purchase amount of US$3,000 million between October 1, 2012, and March 29, 2013.	Neutral
Cyprus	Effective March 28, 2013, restrictions were imposed on banking operations of commercial banks without licenses to carry out transactions for international clients and of Cypriot customers of the licensed banks.	Tightening

Table 7.a (continued)

Country	Change	Type
Egypt	Effective December 30, 2012, the Central Bank of Egypt (CBE) introduced a multiple price auction mechanism to buy and sell foreign exchange with the following rules (1) The CBE sets the bid amounts (not the price). (2) Each bank may submit up to three bids in the auction, for which the total amount is determined by the quota assigned to the bank by the CBE, based on its commercial needs and previous sales in the interbank market. (3) On the auction day, the CBE announces the amount to be offered one hour before to the auction. (4) Once a week, the CBE announces the auction dates for the week. (5) Banks receive a list of priority clients based on strategic needs (foreign investors and clients with commercial needs are given priority). (6) Banks authorized by the CBE may participate in the auction. (7) Auction results are announced to the public through several data service providers, such as Reuters and Bloomberg, as well as on the CBE website.	Neutral
Egypt	Effective January 6, 2013, the following restrictions were imposed on bid-ask spreads quoted by authorized foreign exchange dealers: (1) The client bid rate may range from three piastres (one piastre is one one-hundredth of a pound) below the interbank bid rate to the interbank bid rate (previously, from 150 basis points below the interbank bid rate to the interbank bid rate). (2) The client offer rate must not exceed three piastres above the interbank offer rate (previously, within 50–150 basis points above the interbank rate).	Tightening
Egypt	Effective February 4, 2013, the restrictions regarding bid-ask spreads were revised as follows: (1) The interbank bid-offer rate may be ±1 piastre (one piastre is one one-hundredth of a pound) around the weighted average of the latest auction held by the Central Bank of Egypt. (2) The client bid rate may be between one piastre below the interbank bid rate and the interbank bid rate. (3) The client offer rate (for those with commercial needs) may vary between the interbank offer rate and one piastre above the interbank offer rate. Retail clients pay an additional commission of 1–2 piastres (previously, 0.5–1%) on the offer side.	Tightening
Egypt	Effective February 4, 2013, in the interbank market, banks may place their bids and offers within a band of ±1 piastre (previously, ±0.5%) around the weighted average rate of the most recent foreign exchange auction.	Tightening
Egypt	Effective April 14, 2013, the Central Bank of Egypt announced and held an exceptional auction for the sale of US$600 million. Banks were required to apply with the amount of their clients' outstanding import needs in conformity with the following import commodities: (1) staple commodities (tea, meat, poultry, fish, wheat, oil, milk powder and infant milk, beans, lentils, butter, corn); (2) capital goods spare parts; (3) intermediary production components and raw materials; and (4) pharmaceuticals and vaccines.	Neutral
El Salvador	Effective October 31, 2012, the Board of the Central Reserve Bank approved the Minimum Guidelines for Operations involving Currency Forwards, enabling banks in the system to engage in such operations.	Easing
Fiji	Effective January 1, 2012, authorized banks may write net forward sales contracts up to F$20 million.	Easing
Guatemala	Effective December 28, 2012, the fluctuation margin (added to or subtracted from the five-day moving average of the exchange rate) used to determine whether the Bank of Guatemala may intervene was increased from 0.6% to 0.65%.	Easing
Hungary	Effective February 27, 2012, the Magyar Nemzeti Bank (MNB) terminated the foreign currency sale tenders program. Previously, the MNB operated a program of foreign exchange sale tenders to provide banks with foreign currency to close their open positions arising from early repayment of foreign-currency-denominated mortgages.	Easing
Iraq	Effective February 21, 2012, banks' spread was capped at ID 10 per U.S. dollar over the price at which they can buy foreign exchange at the Central Bank of Iraq auctions.	Tightening
Iraq	Effective April 2, 2012, the limit on banks' cash foreign exchange purchases in the auction was increased from US$250,000 to US$400,000.	Easing
Iraq	Effective April 12, 2012, the amount of foreign exchange licensed money transfer companies and exchange bureaus may purchase was reduced from US$250,000 to US$75,000 a week.	Tightening

Table 7.a (continued)

Country	Change	Type
Iraq	Effective April 12, 2012, the limit on banks' cash foreign exchange purchases in the auction was reduced to US$250,000 from US$400,000.	Tightening
Iraq	Effective June 26, 2012, limits were set on banks' purchases of foreign exchange in the auction for transfers between US$3 million and US$10 million depending on the amount of bank capital.	Tightening
Iraq	Effective June 26, 2012, money transfer companies may not transfer foreign exchange for their clients' import transactions.	Tightening
Iraq	Effective June 26, 2012, the limit on banks' cash foreign exchange purchases in the auction was increased to US$1.25 million from US$250,000.	Easing
Iraq	Effective July 10, 2012, the limit on banks' cash foreign exchange purchases in the auction was increased to US$2 million from US$1.25 million.	Easing
Iraq	Effective July 10, 2012, the limits on banks' purchases of foreign exchange in the auction for transfers were increased to between US$5 million and US$15 million from between US$3 million and US$10 million.	Easing
Iraq	Effective October 1, 2012, the limit on banks spreads of ID 10 per U.S. dollar over the price at which they can buy foreign exchange at the Central Bank of Iraq auctions was eliminated.	Easing
Iraq	Effective October 1, 2012, the limits on banks' purchases of foreign exchange in the auction for transfers were eliminated.	Easing
Iraq	Effective October 1, 2012, the limit on banks' cash foreign exchange purchases in the auction was increased to US$4 million from US$2 million.	Easing
Iraq	Effective October 1, 2012, individuals may buy US$5,000 in foreign exchange for any purpose on proof of identity with a passport. Previously, individuals were allowed to buy foreign exchange up to US$10,000 for certain purposes only with supporting documentation.	Tightening
Iraq	Effective February 17, 2013, authorized banks spreads were capped at ID 10 per U.S. dollar over the exchange rate at which banks can buy foreign exchange in the Central Bank of Iraq auctions.	Tightening
Iraq	Effective April 15, 2013, the weekly limits for money transfer companies and money exchange companies were increased to US$450,000 from US$75,000 and to US$300,000 from US$75,000, respectively. These limits may be increased or decreased according to market conditions and the companies' commitment to sell U.S. dollars to citizens.	Easing
Lebanon	Effective June 30, 2013, the Central Bank of Lebanon issued Basic Circular No. 4 of December 7, 2011. It stipulates that category A money dealers must raise their capital to LBP 750 million from LBP 250 million and category B money dealers from LBP 100 million to LBP 250 million—or LBP 500 million if established before December 7, 2011, and 500 million if established on or after December 7, 2011. Money dealers were given until June 30, 2013, to comply. Category A money dealers may deal in cash, transfers, checks, traveler's checks, and precious metals. Category B dealers whose capital was raised to LBP 500 million may deal in cash and traveler's checks up to the equivalent of US$10,000, uncollected traveler's checks, and gold bars not exceeding 1,000 grams. Category B money dealers established before December 7, 2011, may opt to raise their capital to LBP 500 million in order to expand their operations to include the above (BDL Basic Circular No. 4).	Tightening
Lithuania	Effective January 1, 2012, electronic money institutions may perform foreign exchange operations related to the issuance of electronic money and the provision of other payment services.	Easing
Macedonia	Effective October 23, 2012, the Decision on Currency Exchange Operations went into effect. It liberalized certain documentation requirements for licensing of foreign exchange bureaus and additional conditions for operations.	Easing
Moldova	Effective March 1, 2013, the National Bank of Moldova (NBM) launched foreign exchange auctions (in the form of multiple price auctions) for purchases and sales of foreign currency against lei between the NBM and licensed banks through a unique trading platform.	Neutral

Table 7.a (continued)

Country	Change	Type
Myanmar	Effective January 26, 2012, customers may buy or sell in the retail market up to US$10,000, or its equivalent in Singapore dollars, and euros without documentation. For larger amounts, additional documentation may be required. Previously, documentation was required for all transactions.	Easing
Myanmar	Effective February 9, 2012, wholesale private banks authorized to deal in foreign exchange may settle foreign exchange transactions among themselves using foreign exchange accounts at the Central Bank of Myanmar. ADs are allowed to offer larger noncash foreign exchange services to customers and to trade directly with each other in the AD market	Easing
Myanmar	Effective April 2, 2012, the Central Bank of Myanmar began to hold daily two-way multiple price foreign exchange auctions open to AD banks.	Neutral
Myanmar	Effective April 2, 2012, the Central Bank of Myanmar reference rate is used to set the midrate in the retail Thein Phyu market and in the wholesale/interbank market for ADs.	Neutral
Myanmar	Effective April 2, 2012, actual exchange rates quoted by wholesale foreign exchange ADs may vary within ±0.3% of the CBM reference rate, which is the cutoff rate in that day's daily foreign exchange auction.	Tightening
Myanmar	Effective April 2, 2012, private banks licensed as MCs to buy and sell foreign exchange may transact within ±0.8% of the CBM's reference exchange rate.	Easing
Myanmar	Effective October 22, 2012, actual exchange rates quoted by wholesale foreign exchange ADs may vary within ±0.8% (previously, ±0.3%) of the CBM reference rate, which is the cutoff rate in that day's daily foreign exchange auction.	Easing
Pakistan	Effective February 13, 2013, for exchange companies (both category A and B), the spread between the buying and selling rates of foreign currencies may not exceed 25 paisas (Foreign Exchange Circular No. 1 of February 12, 2013).	Tightening
Romania	Effective May 19, 2012, licensing and control of entities performing foreign exchange transactions in cash and cash substitutes, other than those in the area of prudential supervision of the National Bank of Romania (foreign exchange offices), were transferred to the Ministry of Public Finance from the National Bank of Romania under Articles 161 and 17 of Law No. 656/2002 on preventing and sanctioning money laundering and to establish measures to prevent and combat terrorism financing, as amended and supplemented and by repealing Norm No. 4/2005.	Neutral
São Tomé and Príncipe	Effective July 17, 2012, purchases of euros between banks/exchange houses and the public must be at the single rate published by the Central Bank of São Tomé and Príncipe, and no commissions are allowed.	Tightening
São Tomé and Príncipe	Effective July 17, 2012, the Central Bank of São Tomé and Príncipe began charging a 1.5% commission on sales and 0.5% on purchases of euros. The commission applies to direct sales and purchases with commercial banks.	Tightening
São Tomé and Príncipe	Effective July 17, 2012, the commission on foreign exchange sales by banks and exchange houses to the public is capped at 2% for euros and 4% for other currency.	Tightening
São Tomé and Príncipe	Effective December 17, 2012, access to foreign exchange from the Central Bank of São Tomé and Príncipe was limited to institutions whose net position in the transaction currency is less than 12% of qualified capital and net position in total foreign currency is less than 25% of qualified capital. Institutions must comply with the central bank's regulations on bank liquidity and capital adequacy. Financial institutions may have access to the central bank's facilities regardless of the above conditions if the foreign exchange is for importation of goods and services during a crisis or for the importation of fuel.	Tightening
Serbia	Effective January 1, 2012, the period during which exchange bureaus must transfer any excess amount of dinars to their current account with a bank was increased to within seven working days from within the same day or not later than the following working day (Decision on Terms and Conditions for Performing Exchange Operations, RS Official Gazette No. 93/2011).	Easing
Serbia	Effective January 1, 2012, the threshold that determines the excess amount of dinars exchange bureaus must transfer to their current account with a bank was decreased to double from triple the average amount of dinars used for the purchase of foreign cash in the month with the highest purchase in the preceding 12 months (Decision on Terms and Conditions for Performing Exchange Operations, RS Official Gazette No. 93/2011).	Tightening

Table 7.a (continued)

Country	Change	Type
Sierra Leone	Effective January 23, 2013, the weekly auction amount was reduced to US$0.70 million from US$1 million.	Neutral
Sri Lanka	Effective March 1, 2012, forward contracts for the sale and/or purchase of foreign exchange between ADs and their clients were limited to 90 days. Such contracts may be concluded only for payments and receipts in foreign exchange connected with established transactions for trade in goods and services and allowable capital transactions.	Tightening
Sri Lanka	Effective January 2, 2013, the 90-day limit on the maturity of forward foreign exchange contracts introduced March 1, 2012, was eliminated.	Easing
Sudan	Effective April 5, 2012, as a temporary arrangement, each client in the foreign exchange market was allowed only one foreign currency check not exceeding US$100,000 in the clearinghouse.	Tightening
Sudan	Effective June 24, 2012, the maximum allowed bid-ask spread was raised to 0.5% from 0.4% in all currencies.	Easing
Sudan	Effective November 7, 2012, exchange bureaus may not buy foreign exchange from the Central Bank of Sudan.	Tightening
Suriname	Effective October 29, 2012, commercial banks and exchange bureaus are licensed by the Central Bank of Suriname, in accordance with the Money Transaction Offices Supervision Act 2012. The Act broadens the tools to regulate exchange bureaus and the Central Bank of Suriname is drafting guidelines to implement this Act. Previously, exchange bureaus were also licensed by the Ministry of Trade.	Tightening
Trinidad and Tobago	Effective May 31, 2012, in addition to the predetermined foreign exchange allocation at a price set by the Central Bank of Trinidad and Tobago (CBTT), authorized dealers may bid at auction for CBTT intervention funds. Although it is a multiple price auction, bids must be within 1% of the CBTT rate for the allocation system. Auctions are held about once a month.	Neutral
Turkey	Effective January 2, 2012, the Central Bank of the Republic of Turkey extended the maturity of foreign exchange deposits borrowed by banks in the interbank market from one week to one month.	Easing
Turkey	Effective January 6, 2012, in order to support additional monetary tightening, the Central Bank of the Republic of Turkey began to conduct intraday foreign exchange selling auctions as necessary. A ceiling of US$50 million was set for total volume of foreign exchange sold.	Neutral
Turkey	Effective January 25, 2012, the Central Bank of the Republic of Turkey suspended the regular foreign exchange selling auctions, but retained the option to hold intraday foreign exchange selling auctions, with a maximum daily amount of US$500 million.	Neutral
Turkey	Effective December 25, 2012, the maturity of the foreign exchange deposits banks may borrow from the Central Bank of the Republic of Turkey was decreased from one month to one week. The lending rates for Central Bank of the Republic of Turkey transactions were raised from 4.5% to 10.0% for U.S. dollars and from 5.5% to 10.0% for euros.	Tightening
Turkey	Effective January 2, 2013, intraday foreign exchange auctions were suspended.	Neutral
Turkey	Effective January 2, 2013, the Central Bank of the Republic of Turkey suspended its activities as an intermediary in the foreign exchange deposit markets.	Neutral
Turkey	Effective June 11, 2013, the Central Bank of the Republic of Turkey announced that it may hold unsterilized intraday foreign exchange sales auctions or foreign exchange interventions when deemed necessary in order to support short-term additional monetary tightening.	Neutral

Table 7. a (concluded)

Country	Change	Type
Turkey	Effective June 11, 2013, the Central Bank of the Republic of Turkey (CBRT) resumed intraday foreign exchange selling auctions with US$50 million to be sold at each auction, and published the following guidelines: (1) Only banks authorized to operate in Foreign Exchange and Banknotes Markets in the central bank are eligible to participate in intraday auctions. (2) The number and other details of the auction are posted on Reuters page CBTQ. Following the announcement of the auction, banks may submit their offers within 15 minutes. (3) Offers may be sent via the CBRT Payment Systems Auction System (IhS). (4) Auctions are held under the multiple-price method. (5) The results of the auctions are posted on Reuters page CBTQ within 15 minutes of the deadline for submission of offers. (6) The minimum offer amount is US$1 million and multiples thereof. (7) The maximum offer amount for each bank is limited to 20% of the total auction amount. (8) Banks may not change their offer amounts and/or prices during the auction. (9) The selling amount for each intraday auction is US$50 million and the full amount of offers received is met up to the auction amount. (10) If there is more than one offer at the price at which the auction is finalized, the distribution is made on a pro rata basis. (11) Banks that do not fulfill their obligations arising from the auctions are subject to the sanctions specified in the Implementation Instructions of the Foreign Exchange and Banknotes Markets.	Neutral
Turkey	Effective June 20, 2013, the amount to be sold at each intraday auction is set individually by the Central Bank of the Republic of Turkey and posted on Reuters page CBTQ.	Neutral
Turkey	Effective June 24, 2013, there may be only one intraday foreign exchange selling auction on the days funding is provided from the policy rate, and the auction amount is set at a minimum US$150 million and posted on Reuters page CBTQ at 3:00 p.m.	Neutral
Turkey	Effective July 2, 2013, the minimum amount for the foreign exchange selling auctions was changed from US$150 million to US$50 million, and the maximum bid amount for each bank is limited to 10% (previously 20%) of the total auction amount.	Neutral
Turkey	Effective August 1, 2013, the intraday foreign exchange selling auction time was changed to 4:30 p.m. from 3:00 p.m.	Neutral
Turkmenistan	Effective February 27, 2012, the Regulations for Conducting Exchange Operations by Authorized Credit Institutions in Cash and Noncash Form with Individuals went into effect.	Neutral
Uganda	Effective February 20, 2012, the Bank of Uganda revised the framework for reserve buildup from purchasing a fixed daily amount of US$1.7 million to purchasing between US$1 million and US$2 million daily, in response to sharp fluctuation of the shilling in February 2012.	Neutral
Ukraine	Effective February 17, 2012, authorized banks may engage in swap and forward transactions involving the purchase and sale of bank metals.	Easing
Ukraine	Effective January 1, 2013, foreign exchange transactions up to HRV 50,000 require documentation verifying the identity of a person; larger amounts require physical identification of the individual. Previously, banks and financial institutions purchased foreign exchange from individuals against any document verifying their identity.	Tightening
Uzbekistan	Effective February 1, 2013, foreign exchange operations with residents must take place through conversion operations departments in banks and foreign exchange bureaus. These departments sell foreign exchange to resident individuals by converting sum on the personal bank card of the resident to foreign exchange deposited on an international payments card.	Tightening
Venezuela	Effective March 25, 2013, the Central Bank of Venezuela launched the foreign currency auction with a first offer of US$200 million through the Complementary System to the Administration of Foreign Exchange.	Neutral

Source: AREAER database.

Foreign Exchange Standing Facility, Allocations, Auctions, and Fixing

More than half of IMF member countries (118) report maintaining some type of official facilities by the central bank in the spot foreign exchange market, an increase of three from the previous year. Burundi, which previously held official foreign exchange auctions, stopped using them, whereas Iceland, the Islamic Republic of Iran, Moldova, and South Sudan had central-bank-operated mechanisms in place during the reporting period.

- Almost two-thirds of members with foreign exchange markets fully or partially operated by the central bank reported maintaining a foreign exchange standing facility (76), one less than during the previous reporting period. Such a facility allows market participants to buy foreign exchange from or sell it to the central bank at predetermined exchange rates and is usually instrumental in maintaining a hard or soft peg arrangement. The credibility of such arrangements depends to a large extent on the availability of foreign exchange reserves backing the facility. All countries with currency boards (12), conventional pegs, with the exception of one (44), or crawling pegs (2) have a foreign exchange standing facility. South Sudan, as a newly independent country with a de jure conventional peg exchange rate regime, has a nascent foreign exchange market and is in the process of developing its central bank operations. The remaining 20 countries primarily have stabilized arrangements (9) or other managed arrangements (6) and their foreign exchange markets are often less developed. Egypt reported having eliminated its foreign exchange standing facility.

- There was an increase (by 2) in the number of countries holding official foreign exchange auctions (31), and in a significant majority of those (26) foreign exchange auctions are the only mechanism operated by central banks. Almost half of these countries have exchange rate regimes classified as floating (14), and almost half of the countries with de facto stabilized arrangements hold foreign exchange auctions (8), of which 6 hold only foreign exchange auctions. Auctions have been also used to influence the exchange rate rather than solely to manage foreign reserves. For example, Mexico, the only free floater with a foreign exchange auction in place, has implemented a mechanism involving foreign exchange sales auctions, which are held if the exchange rate depreciates by more than 2 percent since the previous day. Similarly, Turkey held foreign exchange selling auctions while changing the rules and daily limits of auctions multiple times during this reporting period. Overall, there were 45 changes related to auctions across the membership. Iraq and Turkey combined account for more than half of these changes. After suspending regular foreign exchange selling auctions and intraday foreign exchange auctions in January 2012 and January 2013, respectively, Turkey reinstated the mechanism against a backdrop of significant volatility in June 2013. Iraq, on the other hand, had almost an equal number of tightening (6) and easing (8) measures related to the transaction limits on auction participants. Colombia extended daily direct purchase auctions to build up reserves several times. Trinidad and Tobago added foreign exchange (multiple price) auctions to its allocation system operated by the central bank, and Venezuela launched foreign exchange auctions, expanding the mechanisms (foreign exchange standing facility and allocation system) its central bank already had in place. Moldova launched two-way multiple price foreign exchange auctions, and Egypt replaced the foreign exchange standing facility with two-way multiple price auctions. During this period, Burundi discontinued the Marché des Enchères Symétriques en Devises, a platform the central bank used to hold foreign exchange auctions as part of an effort to revamp its foreign exchange market. Hungary discontinued foreign currency sale tenders five months after launching this program to provide banks with liquidity for a specific purpose.[17]

- The number of countries with allocation systems increased by 1 to 31, reaching the same number of countries with foreign exchange auctions. As opposed to countries holding foreign exchange auctions, most of the countries (24) with allocation systems also rely on other mechanisms operated by their central banks. Foreign exchange allocation is often used to provide foreign exchange for strategic imports, such as oil or food, when foreign exchange reserves are scarce. When these arrangements result in rationing, they can give rise to exchange restrictions. The Foreign Exchange Trade Center, operated by Iran's central bank, provides foreign exchange for imports of authorized goods. Similarly, Sudan's central bank sells foreign exchange to commercial banks in accordance with the importance of the imported commodity, with priority on strategic needs. With a nascent foreign exchange market, the Bank of South Sudan attempts to clear the foreign

---

[17] The objective of the foreign exchange auctions was to provide banks with foreign currency to close their open positions arising from early repayment of foreign-currency-denominated mortgages by their clients. Banks could voluntarily participate in the auctions, in which all bids close to prevailing foreign exchange market rates were accepted.

exchange market through weekly allocations, under the nominal anchor of the fixed exchange rate. Malawi no longer allocates foreign exchange to authorized dealers at their request to meet their clients' demand after implementing the revised Guidelines for Foreign Exchange Trading Activities to allow for more market determination of the exchange rate.

- There has been no change in the number (5) or composition of countries holding fixing sessions. Only Belarus and Mauritania continue to operate fixing sessions on a regular basis. As a major conduit for foreign aid flows, Mozambique's central bank channels foreign exchange into the market by holding selling sessions with authorized banks via its software platform. Serbia retains the option of using fixing sessions when necessary to stabilize the foreign exchange market. Although Syria indicated that it held fixing sessions during this reporting period, the extent and regularity of its operations are unknown. Fixing sessions are more characteristic of an early stage of market development, when they help establish a market-clearing exchange rate in a shallow market with less experienced market participants.

Interbank and Retail Foreign Exchange Markets

Two additional countries reported a functioning interbank market: Bosnia and Herzegovina and Comoros. The main types of interbank markets in these 161 countries include over-the-counter markets, brokerage arrangements, and market-making arrangements. Thirty-four members allow operation of all three types of systems.

- Among the countries with a functioning interbank market, more than two-thirds (122), seven more than in the previous year, operate over the counter: 64 of those operate exclusively over the counter; nearly one-half (73) employ a market-making arrangement; and slightly less than one-third (49) allow for intermediation by brokers.

- Over-the-counter operations account for the majority of interbank markets because in a number of economies, particularly small economies, market participants cannot undertake the commitments of a market maker. Burundi established an over-the-counter interbank foreign exchange market, the Marché Interbancaire des Devises, to replace the previous foreign exchange auctions. Over-the-counter foreign exchange markets operate in developed economies as well, where the market is sufficiently liquid to operate without the support of specific arrangements or institutions.

- Six members reported an inactive interbank market.

- Forty-nine members reported using brokers (for example, Republic of Korea and Singapore), three more than in the previous year. El Salvador, Peru, and Russia now report broker participation in the foreign exchange market.

- Seventy-two members reported using market-making agreements in the interbank market, an increase of one since last year. This form of market arrangement is used both in developed economies (such as Switzerland) and developing economies (such as Zambia) and across all types of exchange rate arrangements.

More than two-thirds of the membership reports a framework for foreign exchange bureaus. The majority of these countries impose a licensing requirement, but in a number of them, there are no bureaus in operation. Several changes were implemented with respect to exchange bureaus during the reporting period; these were overwhelmingly tightening. Serbia modified the regulation regarding the excess amount of dinars exchange bureaus are required to transfer into their current accounts with banks by extending the period during which such transfers must be made (easing) but lowering the threshold that defines the excess amount (tightening). The Central Bank of Lebanon issued a circular that requires money dealers dealing in cash, transfers, checks, traveler's checks, and precious metals to raise their capital significantly. In Sudan, exchange bureaus may no longer buy foreign exchange from the central bank. The Central Bank of Suriname became the sole authority for issuance of licenses to commercial banks and exchange bureaus (previously, exchange bureaus were also licensed by the Ministry of Trade). Cyprus imposed restrictions on banking operations of commercial banks but exempted certain licensed banks to allow them to carry out transactions for international clients. In Uzbekistan, conversion by residents of sum to foreign exchange must take place through personal bank cards. Conversion operation departments in banks and foreign exchange bureaus sell foreign exchange to resident individuals by converting sum on the personal bank card of the resident to foreign exchange deposited on an international payment card. Ukraine imposed further identification restrictions, requiring physical identification of individuals for transactions exceeding HRV 50,000. In contrast, in Lithuania, electronic money institutions may now perform foreign exchange operations related to the issuance of electronic money and the provision of other payment services. Macedonia liberalized certain documentation requirements for licensing of foreign exchange bureaus and additional conditions for operations.

Although the majority of members refrain from restricting exchange rate spreads and commissions in the interbank market, several countries imposed new or additional restrictions in this area. Pakistan limited exchange companies' (both category A and B) spreads between the buying and selling rates of foreign currencies to 25 paisas. The Central Bank of São Tomé and Príncipe began charging a 1.5 percent commission on sales and 0.5 percent on purchases of euros and capped the commission on foreign exchange sales by banks and exchange houses to the public at 2 percent for euros and 4 percent for other currencies. Egypt progressively tightened the limits on bid-ask spreads in the interbank and spot markets. On the easing side, Sudan slightly raised the bid-ask spread for the interbank market.

Among the countries reporting controls on interbank foreign exchange pricing are Botswana, China, the Democratic Republic of the Congo, Haiti, and Saudi Arabia. Many of the spread limits are agreed among market participants in the context of market making or other ad hoc agreements. These limitations are generally implemented in the context of fixed or stabilized exchange rate arrangements.

There were several other developments in currency pricing. China widened the interbank trading fluctuation band from ±0.5 percent to ±1 percent around the central parity released on the same day by the China Foreign Exchange Trade System. Myanmar, as part of a transition to a more flexible exchange rate regime, introduced a number of measures in foreign exchange trading in order to unify the multiple exchange rate system by imposing a transaction range of ±0.8 percent around the reference rate for banks' transactions with clients. It later raised the ±0.3 percent limit for interbank trading to ±0.8 percent. The Bank of the Republic of Burundi set a fluctuation margin on foreign currency buying and selling transactions by commercial banks and exchange bureaus of ±1 percent of the reference rate it publishes each morning.

Other Measures

Most of the changes in other measures during the reporting period refer to exchange rate structure (Table 7.b), taxes on foreign exchange transactions (Table 7.c), and forward and swap operations (see Table 7.a).

- Changes related to forward transactions continued to gravitate toward easing (see Table 7.a): there were four easing changes as opposed to one tightening measure. For example, Fiji authorized banks to write net forward sales contracts up to F$20 million. As part of its foreign exchange market liberalization efforts, Ukraine authorized banks to trade in foreign exchange swaps among themselves. El Salvador approved minimum guidelines for operations involving currency forwards, enabling its banks to engage in such operations. Sri Lanka eliminated the limit on the maturity of forward foreign exchange contracts it introduced earlier in the reporting period.

- There were several changes in the number of countries maintaining dual or multiple exchange rate structures (see Table 7.b). Madagascar's exchange rate structure was changed back to dual from unitary after the reinstatement of a preferential exchange rate for oil importers. Similarly, the exchange rate structure of Iran was reclassified as multiple given the implementation of a two-tier exchange rate system, under which imports of food and basic goods receive a preferential exchange rate, in addition to a more depreciated parallel rate offered by the exchange bureaus. Ghana's exchange rate structure was also changed from unitary to dual, since the official rate may differ by more than 2 percent from market rates. In contrast, São Tomé and Príncipe capped the commissions on sales of euros and other currencies and required purchases to be made at a single rate published by the central bank, which caused its exchange rate structure to be classified as unitary. Currently, 24 countries are classified as having more than one exchange rate, of which 17 are dual and 7 multiple. This is a result mainly of specific exchange rates applied for certain transactions or actual or potential deviations of more than 2 percent between official and other exchange rates.

- There were a few changes with respect to foreign exchange taxes (see Table 7.c). Aruba revoked the foreign exchange commission exemption for transactions settled in Netherlands Antilles guilders. Bolivia introduced a foreign exchange tax of 0.7 percent on a temporary basis for 36 months, and Ecuador increased the tax on transfers abroad from 2 percent to 5 percent. Responding to changes in capital inflows, Brazil took a series of steps that slightly eased the taxing of foreign-exchange-related transactions. Overall, 32 countries (the same as the previous year) tax foreign exchange transactions. On the other hand, only two countries (Serbia and Sudan) have foreign exchange subsidies in place benefiting certain export sectors.

- Finally, a series of neutral changes were recorded (see Table 7.b). Myanmar implemented a process for redemption of foreign exchange certificates to be used for payments until a deadline. The government of Zambia rebased the kwacha by removing three zeros. Venezuela took several steps to improve its multiple exchange rate structure.

Table 7. b. Changes in Currency and Exchange Rate Structures, January 1, 2012–August 31, 2013

Country	Change	Type
Bhutan	Effective May 1, 2012, Indian rupees were no longer freely issued over the counter. All current international transactions denominated in rupees were streamlined to reflect the legal status of the rupee as a foreign currency.	Tightening
Ghana	Effective July 2, 2012, the exchange rate structure was changed from unitary to dual because the Bank of Ghana uses a reference rate for certain official transactions. This rate does not involve a mechanism to ensure that it does not differ from the prevailing market rate by more than 2%, thus giving rise to a multiple currency practice.	Tightening
Islamic Republic of Iran	Effective September 24, 2012, the authorities adopted a two-tier exchange rate system, under which the Central Bank of Iran maintains a more appreciated interbank exchange rate for imports of food and basic goods and offers a second rate at the Foreign Exchange Trade Center for imports of authorized goods.	Tightening
Islamic Republic of Iran	Effective September 24, 2012, the exchange rate structure was changed to multiple from unitary because in addition to the two-tier exchange rate system, under which the Central Band of Iran maintains a more appreciated interbank exchange rate for imports of food and basic goods and offers a second exchange rate at the Foreign Exchange Trade Center for imports of authorized goods, a more depreciated parallel rate is offered at the exchange rate bureaus.	Tightening
Madagascar	Effective March 13, 2012, the preferential exchange rate for oil importers (MGA 2,000 per U.S. dollar) was reinstated.	Tightening
Madagascar	Effective March 3, 2012, as a result of the preferential exchange rate used for oil imports, the exchange rate structure was changed from unitary to dual.	Tightening
Myanmar	Effective April 2, 2012, the official exchange rate was replaced with a reference rate for foreign exchange transactions with the government. This reference rate is used to set the Thein Phyu midrate, which generally remains within 0.8% of the reference rate but occasionally may differ by more than 2% from the other rates.	Neutral
Myanmar	Effective April 1, 2013, a process for redemption of foreign exchange certificates was established. Under the redemption, such certificates could be used for payments until June 30, 2013.	Neutral
São Tomé and Príncipe	As a result of the Central Bank of São Tomé and Príncipe (BCSTP) regulations, which set a maximum commission of 2% on sales of euros and 4% on sales of other currencies, and required purchases of euros to be made at the single rate published daily by the BCSTP, with no commissions, the exchange rate structure was changed to unitary from multiple, effective July 17, 2012.	Easing

Table 7.b (concluded)

Country	Change	Type
Sudan	Effective June 24, 2012, Sudan adopted a new multiple exchange rate regime including (1) a central rate of SDG 4.42 per U.S. dollar that also applies to fuel imports, the payment of government obligations, and customs valuation; (2) a subsidized rate for wheat of SDG 2.9 per U.S. dollar; (3) a gold exchange rate used by the Central Bank of Sudan (CBOS) in its gold transactions; and (4) a managed float rate used mainly by commercial banks and exchange bureaus. The managed float rate applies to all other transactions and has three components: (1) an indicative rate; (2) a variable incentive premium set by the CBOS (currently 15%); and (3) a flexibility factor that allows banks to deviate from the average of the indicative rate and the incentive by ±4% (previously ±3%).	Neutral
Ukraine	Effective June 18, 2012, although the multiple currency practice arising from the official foreign exchange auction has been eliminated, the exchange rate structure is classified as dual, because of the potential difference in exchange rates for certain government transactions and the market exchange rate.	Tightening
Venezuela	Effective February 8, 2013, the official bolívar–U.S. dollar exchange rate was devalued to Bs 6.30 from Bs 4.30 per U.S. dollar.	Neutral
Venezuela	Effective February 8, 2013, the implicit rate of Bs 5.30 per U.S. dollar that applied to purchases and sales in bolívares of foreign-currency-denominated securities issued by Venezuela, its decentralized entities, and other entities in the Transaction System for Foreign-Currency-Denominated Securities operated by the Central Bank of Venezuela was discontinued.	Neutral
Venezuela	Effective March 25, 2013, the Transaction System for Foreign-Currency-Denominated Securities was replaced with the Complementary System to the Administration of Foreign Exchange to complement the Commission for the Administration of Currency Exchange system, which supplies foreign exchange at the official rate of Bs 6.30 per U.S. dollar. Access to the Complementary System to the Administration of Foreign Exchange is restricted to importers selling food, medicine, and other basic goods.	Neutral
Zambia	Effective January 23, 2012, the government of Zambia approved the recommendation of the Bank of Zambia board of directors to rebase the kwacha.	Neutral
Zambia	Effective January 1, 2013, the kwacha was rebased by removing three zeros. The rebased kwacha circulated alongside the old currency for six months.	Neutral

Source: AREAER database.

Table 7.c. Changes in Exchange Subsidies and Exchange Taxes, January 1, 2012–August 31, 2013

Country	Change	Type
Aruba	Effective January 1, 2012, the exemption for foreign exchange commissions for payments settled in Netherlands Antillean guilders was revoked (AB 2011 No. 76).	Tightening
Bolivia	Effective December 5, 2012, a tax throughout the national territory was established (Supreme Decree No. 1423 of September 22, 2012) on a temporary basis for 36 months on the sale of foreign currency. The rate is 0.7% of the assessed tax base. For financial and nonbank entities, the assessed base is the sum of all foreign currency sales expressed in local currency. The taxable base for exchange bureaus is 50% of the sum of all foreign currency sales expressed in local currency. The sale of foreign currency by financial institutions to the Central Bank of Bolivia is exempt.	Tightening
Brazil	Effective February 29, 2012, the 6% IOF rate maximum maturity was increased from 720 days to 1,080 days for inflows related to external loans.	Tightening

Table 7.c (concluded)

Country	Change	Type
Brazil	Effective February 29, 2012, the IOF rate was reduced from 2% to zero for settlements of simultaneously contracted foreign exchange transactions after December 1, 2011, related to inflows from cancellation of depository receipts invested in the acquisition of stocks in the stock market.	Easing
Brazil	Effective March 12, 2012, the maximum maturity of external loans subject to the 6% IOF rate was increased from 1,080 days to 1,800 days.	Tightening
Brazil	Effective June 14, 2012, the maximum maturity of external loans subject to the 6% IOF rate was decreased from 1,800 days to 720 days.	Easing
Brazil	Effective December 5, 2012, the maximum maturity of external loans subject to the 6% rate was decreased from 720 days to 360 days.	Easing
Ecuador	Effective January 1, 2012, the tax on transfers abroad was increased from 2% to 5%.	Tightening

Source: AREAER database.

Member Countries' Obligations and Status under Article VIII

This section provides an overview of the acceptance by most IMF members of the obligations of Article VIII, Sections 2(a), 3, and 4, of the Articles of Agreement and of other members' use of the transitional arrangements of Article XIV. It also describes restrictive exchange measures—namely, exchange restrictions and multiple currency practices (MCPs) subject to IMF jurisdiction under Articles VIII and XIV and measures imposed by members for national and/or international security reasons. Further, this section refers to changes in restrictive exchange measures in 2012 and to members' positions as reported in the latest IMF staff reports as of December 31, 2012.

In accepting the obligations of Article VIII, Sections 2(a), 3, and 4, members agree not to impose restrictions on payments and transfers for current international transactions or engage in discriminatory currency arrangements or MCPs. Out of 188 members of the IMF, 168 have accepted Article VIII status. Of these Article VIII members, the number of those maintaining restrictive exchange measures increased by 4 to 34 in 2012.[18]

IMF staff reports indicate that, among the members with Article XIV status, Afghanistan, Liberia, and Tuvalu do not maintain any exchange restrictions or MCPs. Angola, Bhutan, and Syria maintain exchange measures under both Article VIII and Article XIV. Bosnia and Herzegovina, Burundi, Eritrea, Ethiopia, Iraq, Maldives, Myanmar, Nigeria, São Tomé and Príncipe, and Turkmenistan maintain exchange measures under Article VIII only, and Albania maintains exchange measures under Article XIV only. The exchange regimes of Kosovo and South Sudan are under IMF staff review. The exchange regime of Somalia will be reviewed as circumstances permit.

Restrictive Exchange Measures

Exchange Restrictions and/or multiple currency practices

The overall stance of restrictive exchange measures tightened somewhat in 2012 as both the total number of measures maintained and the number of members maintaining them increased. The total number of restrictions or MCPs maintained by members increased by 7 to 102 in 2012, reversing a decline of 5 in 2011. While the decline in restrictive exchange measures in 2011 was attributable to Article XIV members, both Article VIII and Article XIV members contributed to the increase in 2012. The number of members that maintained restrictive exchange measures, which increased by 1 in 2011, further increased by 4 to a total of 48 in 2012. This reflected the reporting of exchange measures by members with Article VIII status (Ghana, Hungary, Iceland, Ukraine). Taking account of both the increases in the number of restrictive exchange measures and the total number of members that maintained such measures, the average number of measures per member maintaining such measures remained almost the same at just above 2 in 2012.

---

[18] The AREAER does not indicate whether the IMF has approved such measures.

The average number of restrictions or MCPs maintained by Article XIV members is significantly higher than the figure for Article VIII members. With a slight increase in the number of restrictive exchange measures, the average number of measures for Article XIV members reached 3.9. In contrast, for Article VIII members that maintain exchange measures, broadly commensurate increases in the number of measures and members maintaining such measures caused the average number of measures to remain the same at 1.4.

Changes in restrictive exchange measures maintained by members in 2012 were diverse in nature. For example, among Article XIV countries, São Tomé and Príncipe eliminated an MCP arising from multiple exchange markets with no mechanism to prevent spreads among effective exchange rates in the spot market to diverge more than 2 percent at any time. Further, an IMF staff review found that Myanmar maintained restrictions, including advance import deposit requirements, a 100 percent margin requirement for imports, general restrictions on the making of payments and transfers for invisible transactions, and official action imposing additional costs for exchange transactions. Myanmar also maintained MCPs, including official action giving rise to multiple effective exchange rates and broken cross rates. Among Article VIII countries, Belarus imposed advance import deposit requirements to reduce stress on the balance of payments. To increase the effectiveness of capital controls, Iceland placed limits on remittances of the amortized principal on bonds and the indexed portion of amortization. Ghana maintained an MCP in the form of a special reference rate for certain official imports. Hungary adopted an MCP in the form of an exchange plan that involved multiple effective exchange rates for spot transactions with no mechanism to prevent spreads among effective exchange rates in the spot market from diverging more than 2 percent at any time. This measure was related to a policy to help debtors in foreign currency mortgages who had been adversely affected by the depreciation of the forint vis-à-vis other currencies in which mortgage loans were extended in Hungary. Ukraine maintained two MCPs in the form of a preferential official exchange rate for certain government transactions and, to safeguard reserves and prevent capital flight, a requirement to surrender gains on foreign exchange purchased but not used.

Table 8 shows the distribution of exchange measures under IMF jurisdiction by type and by status of members during the period 2010–12. Because of the disaggregation of the wide variety of measures, the number of measures in each category is relatively low.

Though the number of restrictions on payments for imports increased by 3 to 9 in 2012, they form a small fraction of exchange measures as a whole. They include advance import deposits or margin requirements that increase the effective cost of imports (Myanmar, Sudan), restrictions on advance payments that seek to minimize the delay between payment and performance (Belarus, Swaziland), and restrictive administrative rules with respect to imports (Bhutan, Ethiopia).

Restrictions on payments for invisibles declined by 1, to 21 in 2012, leaving such restrictions at about a fifth of total exchange measures. These restrictions reflect members' policy of reducing the use of foreign exchange for transactions considered to have low priority and of restraining large transfers of investment income, in part to encourage reinvestment. Restrictions on payments for invisibles that typically affect individuals include limits on educational allowances (Angola), medical expenses (Angola), travel abroad (Angola, Bhutan, Eritrea, Sudan), and interest on nonresident domestic currency deposits (Bangladesh). Restrictions that affect the business sector include constraints on the remittance of investment income in the form of a tax clearance requirement (Ethiopia, Fiji, São Tomé and Príncipe), an exchange tax on profits (Colombia), limitations on the remittance of interest on frozen foreign currency deposits (Bosnia) and on bonds (Iceland), limitations on the remittance of profits and dividends, whether realized in foreign or domestic currency (Angola, Eritrea, Iran), a requirement that foreign exchange earnings cover investment income remittances (foreign exchange balancing, Bhutan), or requirements to clear debts to the government before the transfer of profit abroad (Iraq).

Members maintain other transaction-specific restrictions. The definition of a current international transaction in Article XXX(d) of the IMF's Articles of Agreement includes the amortization of external loans and bonds. Thus, restrictions on such amortization (Ethiopia, Iceland, India) fall within the jurisdiction of the IMF. Some members maintain restrictions on unrequited transfers, including limits on the transfer by nonresidents of salaries and wages (Nepal), a requirement to clear debts with the government prior to remitting wages (Iraq), and limitations on other private transfers (Angola, Bhutan). Limits are maintained on the transferability of balances in frozen foreign exchange accounts in the former Yugoslavia (Bosnia and Herzegovina, Montenegro, Serbia). Unsettled debit balances in bilateral or regional payments, barter, or clearing arrangements give rise to exchange restrictions (Albania, Democratic Republic of the Congo, India, Iraq, Syria, Zimbabwe). The incidence of unsettled balances has remained at 7 since 2010, suggesting challenges in settling balances from inoperative arrangements.

Restrictions of general applicability remained in the range of 17 to 19 measures during 2010–12, accounting for about a fifth of total exchange measures. Included in this category are measures involving administrative allocation of foreign exchange, rationing, and undue delay in the provision of foreign exchange (Eritrea, Maldives, Myanmar, Syria), limits on payments above a threshold (Fiji), tax clearance certificate requirements (Iraq), exchange taxes that constitute restrictions but not MCPs (Angola, Aruba, Gabon), and a requirement to surrender export earnings for access to foreign exchange (Colombia).

The number of MCPs, which broadly constituted about a third of exchange measures during 2010–12, increased by 2 to 34 in 2012. Official action that of itself gives rise to a spread of more than 2 percent between buying and selling rates for spot exchange transactions, or in the context of multiprice auction systems when the system established by official action has no mechanism to prevent such a spread, is considered an MCP. MCPs come in a variety of forms. Differentials between official and market rates triggered by official action, which form the largest subset of MCPs, increased by 3, to 21. Such MCPs typically arise from the mandatory use of a specific exchange rate for certain transactions or from maintaining an unrealistic exchange rate level that channels foreign exchange transactions to a parallel market with a more depreciated exchange rate. More Article VIII members (Democratic Republic of the Congo, Georgia, Ghana, Guinea, Hungary, Kyrgyz Republic, Malawi, Mongolia, Suriname, Ukraine) maintain actions that give rise to these differentials than do Article XIV members (Burundi, Eritrea, Maldives, Myanmar, Syria). Other measures giving rise to MCPs are exchange taxes (Angola, Colombia, Eritrea), margin requirements (Sudan), non-interest-bearing advance import deposits (Syria), exchange guarantees (Tunisia), and multiple price foreign exchange auctions (Angola, Mongolia, Nigeria, Sierra Leone). Such auctions are often implemented until a well-functioning interbank market develops.

Table 9 provides descriptions of restrictive exchange measures by members as indicated in the latest IMF staff reports as of December 31, 2012. Excluded from Table 9 are member countries that have not consented to publication of such measures described in unpublished IMF staff reports.

Exchange measures maintained for security reasons

Some members maintain measures imposed solely for national and/or internal security reasons, which could give rise to exchange restrictions under IMF jurisdiction and as such require IMF approval under Article VIII, Section 2(a). However, because the IMF does not provide a suitable forum for discussion of political and military considerations leading to measures of this kind, it established a special procedure for notification and approval of such measures.[19] In total, 14 members notified the IMF of measures introduced solely for security reasons during 2012; 10 members did so during January–August 2013. For the most part, notification was from advanced economies. In general, the restrictions involved take the form of financial sanctions to combat financial terrorism or financial sanctions against certain governments, entities, and individuals in accordance with UN Security Council resolutions or EU regulations.

---

[19] See Decision No. 144-(52/51) in Selected Decisions and Selected Documents of the International Monetary Fund, Issue 36 (Washington: IMF, 2012).

Table 8. Exchange Restrictions and Multiple Currency Practices, January 1, 2012–December 31, 2012

	Member under								
	Article XIV Status			Article VIII Status			Total		
	2010	2011	2012	2010	2011	2012	2010	2011	2012
Total number of restrictions maintained by members[1]	57	52	54	43	43	48	100	95	102
Restrictions on payments for imports	5	4	6	2	2	3	7	6	9
Advance import deposit and margin requirements			2	1	1	1	1	1	3
Restrictions on advance payments	1			1	1	2	2	1	2
Requirement to balance imports with export earnings	1	1	1				1	1	1
Restrictive rules on the issuance of import permits	1	1	1				1	1	1
Tax clearance requirements	1	1	1				1	1	1
Other	1	1	1				1	1	1
Restrictions on payments for invisibles	17	16	15	7	6	6	24	22	21
Education	1	1	1				1	1	1
Medical services	1	1	1				1	1	1
Travel services	4	4	3	2	1	1	6	5	4
Income on investment	8	8	8	5	5	5	13	13	13
Tax clearance requirement	2	2	2	1	1	1	3	3	3
Exchange tax on profits				1	1	1	1	1	1
Interest on deposits and bonds	1	1	1	2	2	2	3	3	3
Profits and dividends	3	3	3	1	1	1	4	4	4
Foreign exchange balancing for profit remittances	1	1	1				1	1	1
Clearance of debts to government to remit profits	1	1	1				1	1	1
Other	3	2	2				3	2	2
Restrictions on amortization on external loans	1	1	1	1	1	3	2	2	4
Restrictions on unrequited transfers	5	4	3		1	1	5	5	4
Wages and salaries	1	1			1	1	1	2	1
Clearance of debt to government to remit wages	1	1	1				1	1	1
Family remittances	1						1		
Other	2	2	2				2	2	2
Nonresident accounts	3	2	2	3	2	2	6	4	4
Transferability of frozen or blocked deposits	1	1	1	3	2	2	4	3	3
Limits on use of foreign currency accounts	1	1	1				1	1	1
Convertibility of nonresident domestic currency deposits	1						1		
Restrictions arising from bilateral or regional payment, barter, or clearing arrangements: Unsettled debit balances	3	3	3	4	4	4	7	7	7
Restrictions with general applicability	9	8	10	9	9	9	18	17	19
Administered allocations, rationing and undue delay	4	4	5	3	3	3	7	7	8
Payments above a threshold	1			1	1	1	2	1	1

Table 8 (concluded)

| | Member under | | | | | | | | |
| | Article XIV Status | | | Article VIII Status | | | Total | | |
	2010	2011	2012	2010	2011	2012	2010	2011	2012
Tax clearance certificates	1	1	1				1	1	1
Exchange taxes	1	1	1	3	3	3	4	4	4
Surrender of export earnings to have access to foreign exchange				1	1	1	1	1	1
Other	2	2	3	1	1	1	3	3	4
Multiple currency practices	14	14	14	17	18	20	31	32	34
Exchange taxes	4	4	4	1	1	1	5	5	5
Exchange subsidies				1	1		1	1	
Multiple price auctions	2	2	2	2	2	2	4	4	4
Differentials between official, commercial, and parallel rates	7	7	7	10	11	14	17	18	21
Margin requirements				1	1	1	1	1	1
Non-interest-bearing blocked accounts				1	1	1	1	1	1
Non-interest-bearing advance import deposits	1	1	1				1	1	1
Exchange rate guarantees				1	1	1	1	1	1
Memorandum items:									
Average number of restrictions per member	3.8	3.7	3.9	1.5	1.4	1.4	2.3	2.2	2.1
Number of countries with restrictions	15	14	14	28	30	34	43	44	48

Sources: AREAER database and IMF staff reports.

[1] Includes 188 members and three territories: Aruba, Curaçao and Sint Maarten (all Netherlands) and Hong Kong SAR (China).

Table 9. Exchange Restrictions and/or Multiple Currency Practices by Country, as of December 31, 2012

Country[1]	Exchange Restrictions and/or Multiple Currency Practices[2]
Albania	The IMF staff report on the 2012 Article IV Consultations with Albania states that, as of November 19, 2012, Albania still avails itself of the transitional arrangements under Article XIV and maintained an exchange restriction in the form of outstanding debit balances on inoperative bilateral payments agreements, which were in place before Albania became an IMF member. These relate primarily to debt in nonconvertible and formerly nonconvertible currencies. The IMF staff is currently assessing Albania's exchange system for potential exchange restrictions and multiple currency practices. (Country Report No. 13/7)
Angola	The IMF staff report for the 2012 Article IV Consultation and First Post-Program Monitoring with Angola states that, as of July 2, 2012, Angola maintained exchange measures pursuant to the transitional arrangements under Article XIV, and a number of measures subject to IMF jurisdiction under Article VIII. The measures maintained pursuant to Article XIV are (1) limits on the availability of foreign exchange for invisible transactions, such as travel, medical, or educational allowances; and (2) limits on unrequited transfers to foreign-based individuals and institutions. In addition, Angola maintained two exchange restrictions subject to IMF jurisdiction under Article VIII, Section 2. These are (1) limits on the remittances of dividends and profits from foreign investments that do not exceed US$1,000,000; and (2) the discriminatory application of the 0.015% stamp tax on foreign exchange operations. Angola also maintained two multiple currency practices arising from: (1) the Dutch foreign exchange auction; and (2) the discriminatory application of the 0.015% stamp tax on foreign exchange operations that are subject to approval under Article VIII, Section 3. (Country Report No. 12/215)
Aruba	The IMF staff report for the 2010 Article IV consultation with the Kingdom of the Netherlands—Aruba states that, as of October 7, 2010, Aruba maintained a foreign exchange restriction arising from the foreign exchange tax on payments by residents to nonresidents. This tax, which amounts to 1.3% of the transaction value, was introduced when Aruba was part of the Netherlands Antilles to generate revenue for the government. (Country Report No. 10/334)
Bangladesh	The IMF staff report for the 2011 Article IV consultation with Bangladesh states that, as of October 17, 2011, Bangladesh maintained an exchange restriction on the convertibility and transferability of proceeds of current international transactions in nonresident taka accounts. (Country Report No. 11/314)
Belarus	The IMF staff report on the Third Post-Program Monitoring Discussion with Belarus states that, as of November 28, 2012, the authorities lifted some of the earlier introduced administrative controls, including the ban on the purchase of foreign exchange for certain import payments in excess of €50,000. However, based on currently available information, Belarus continues to maintain restrictions on the availability of foreign exchange for advance payments for imports. The IMF staff is currently reviewing the jurisdictional implications of the new regime and the remaining foreign exchange controls.
Bhutan	The IMF staff report for the 2011 Article IV consultation with Bhutan states that, as of May 13, 2011, Bhutan maintained exchange restrictions subject to IMF approval under Article VIII, Section 2(a). (Country Report No. 11/123)
Bosnia	The IMF staff report for the 2012 Article IV Consultation with Bosnia and Herzegovina, states that, as of September 12, 2012, Bosnia and maintained restrictions on the transferability of balances and interest accrued on frozen foreign currency deposits, subject to IMF jurisdiction under Article VIII. (Country Report No. 12/282)
Burundi	The IMF staff report for the 2012 Article IV Consultation, First Review under the Three-Year Arrangement under the Extended Credit Facility states that, as of July 16, 2012, Burundi maintained one multiple currency practice that is inconsistent with Article VIII, Section 2(a): the exchange rate used for government transactions differ by more than 2% from market exchange rates. (Country Report No. 12/226)
Colombia	The IMF staff report for the 2011 Article IV consultation with Colombia states that, as of July 7, 2011, Colombia maintained two exchange measures subject to IMF approval under Article VIII: (1) a multiple currency practice and an exchange restriction arising from a tax on outward remittances of nonresident profits earned before 2007 and that have been retained in the country for less than five years; and (2) an exchange restriction arising from the special regime for the hydrocarbon sector, in which branches of foreign corporations are required to either surrender their export proceeds to the authorities or agree to a government limitation on their access to the foreign exchange market. (Country Report No. 11/224)

Table 9 (continued)

Country[1]	Exchange Restrictions and/or Multiple Currency Practices[2]
Democratic Republic of the Congo	The IMF staff report for the 2012 Article IV Consultation with the Democratic Republic of the Congo (DRC) states that, as of September 6, 2012, the DRC maintained measures that give rise to one exchange rate restriction and one multiple currency practice subject to IMF approval. The exchange restriction involves an outstanding net debt position against other contracting members under the inoperative regional payments agreement with the Economic Community of the Great Lakes Countries. The multiple currency practice relates to a fixed exchange rate set quarterly applying to transactions through a bilateral payments agreement with Zimbabwe. (Country Report No. 13/94)
Ethiopia	The IMF staff report for the 2012 Article IV Consultations states that, as of September 29, 2012, Ethiopia maintained four restrictions on the payments and transfers for current international transactions, which relate to (1) the tax certification requirement for repatriation of dividend and other investment income; (2) restrictions on repayment of legal external loans and supplies and foreign partner credits; (3) rules for issuance of import permits by commercial banks; and (4) the requirement to provide a clearance certificate from National Bank of Ethiopia (NBE) to obtain import permits. These restrictions are inconsistent with Article VIII, Section 2(a), of the IMF's Articles of Agreement. The IMF staff is continuing to assess whether a general finance and economic cooperation agreement signed between the government of Ethiopia and China in 2006 gives rise to exchange restrictions under Article VIII. (Country Report No. 12/287)
Fiji	The IMF staff report for the 2011 Article IV Consultations states that, as of January 06, 2012 Fiji maintained an exchange restriction subject to Article VIII arising from the Fiji Revenue and Customs Authority tax certification requirements before foreign companies can remit profits abroad and from limits on large payments (e.g., oil imports and dividends repatriation of foreign banks). (Country Report No. 12/44)
Gabon	The IMF staff report on the 2010 Article IV Consultations states that, as of February 3, 2011, owing to the imposition of a tax on all wire transfers, including for making payments and transfers for current international transactions, Gabon maintained an exchange restriction subject to IMF approval under Article VIII, Section 2(a), of the Articles of Agreement. (Country Report No. 11/97)
Georgia	The IMF staff report on the Request for a Stand-by Arrangement and an Arrangement under the Standby Credit Facility states that, as of March 29, 2012, the Georgia government uses the official exchange rate for budget and tax accounting purposes as well as for all payments between the government and enterprises and other legal entities, and for foreign exchange transactions with the National Bank of Georgia. The official rate is defined as the average of the previous day's market transaction rates, and may thus differ by more than 2% from the freely determined market rate, which gives rise to a multiple currency practice. In practice, the official and market rates have never differed by more than 2% since the introduction of foreign exchange auctions in March 2009. (Country Report No. 12/98)
Ghana	The IMF staff report for the Sixth and Seventh Reviews Under the Three-year Arrangement Under the Extended Credit Facility states that as of July 2, 2012, Ghana maintained a multiple currency practice, arising from a special reference rate for certain official transactions, subject to IMF approval (Country Report No. 12/201).
Guinea	The IMF staff report on a First Review under the Three-Year Arrangement under the Extended Credit Facility with Guinea states that, as of September 12, 2012, Guinea maintained a multiple currency practice, as the value of the official rate lags the weighted average commercial bank rate on which it is based by one day. (Country Report No. 12/301)
Hungary	The IMF staff report for the 2011 Article IV Consultations and the Second Post-Program Monitoring Discussion states that as of January 4, 2012, Hungary maintained multiple currency practices subject to the IMF's approval under Article VIII, Section 3 arising from the establishment by the Magyar Nemzeti Bank of a foreign exchange scheme that involves a multiplicity of effective exchange rates for spot transactions without a mechanism to ensure that such rates will not deviate among each other by more than 2%. (Country Report No. 12/13)
Iceland	The IMF staff report for the 2012 Article IV Consultation and First Post-Program Monitoring Discussion with Iceland states that, as of March 26, 2012, Iceland maintained exchange restrictions arising from limitations imposed on the conversion and transfer of (1) interest on bonds (whose transfer the foreign exchange rules apportion depending on the period of the holding), (2) amortized principal on bonds, and (3) the indexed portion of principal on bonds. (Country Report No. 12/89)

Table 9 (continued)

Country[1]	Exchange Restrictions and/or Multiple Currency Practices[2]
India	The IMF staff report for the 2012 Article IV Consultation with India states that, as of April 12, 2012, India maintained the following restrictions on the making of payments and transfers for current international transactions, which are subject to IMF approval under Article VIII, Section 2(a): restrictions related to the nontransferability of balances under the India-Russia debt agreement; restrictions arising from unsettled balances under inoperative bilateral payments arrangements with two eastern European countries; and a restriction on the transfer of amortization payments on loans by nonresident relatives. (Country Report No. 13/37)
Islamic Republic of Iran	The IMF staff report for the 2011 Article IV consultation with the Islamic Republic of Iran states that, as of July 6, 2011, Iran maintained one exchange restriction and a multiple currency practice subject to IMF jurisdiction under Article VIII, Sections 2(a) and 3. The exchange restriction arises from limitations on the transferability of rial profits from certain investments under the Foreign Investment Promotion and Protection Act and from limitations on other investment-related current international payments under this act. The multiple currency practice arises from the budget subsidies for foreign exchange purchases in connection with payments of certain Letter of Credits opened prior to March 21, 2002, under the previous multiple exchange rate system. (Country Report No. 11/241)
Iraq	The IMF staff report for the Second Review under the Stand-By Arrangement states that as of March 7, 2011, Iraq maintained four measures (plus one exchange restriction maintained for national or international security) that have been identified to give rise to exchange restrictions subject to IMF approval: (1) the requirement to pay all obligations and debts to the government before proceeds of investments of investors and salaries and other compensation of non-Iraqi employees may be transferred out of Iraq, (2) the requirement to submit a tax certificate and a letter of non-objection stating that the companies do not owe any taxes to the government before non-Iraqi companies may transfer proceeds of current international transactions out of the country, (3) the requirement that before non-Iraqis may transfer proceeds in excess of ID 15 million out of Iraq the banks are required to give due consideration of legal obligations of these persons with respect to official entities, which must be settled before allowing any transfer, and (4) an Iraqi balance owed to Jordan under an inoperative bilateral payments agreement. (Country Report No. 11/75)
Kosovo	The IMF staff report for the 2011 Article IV Consultations with Kosovo states that as of June 22, 2011, the IMF staff is in the process of assessing whether Kosovo imposes exchange restrictions and/or multiple currency practice subject to IMF jurisdiction. (Country Report No. 11/210)
Kyrgyz Republic	The IMF staff report on the Third Review under the Three Year Arrangement under the Extended Credit Facility states that, as of November 15, 2012, the Kyrgyz Republic maintained a multiple currency practice, which predates the arrangement, arising from the use of the official exchange rate for government transactions. The official rate may differ by more than 2% from market rates because it is based on the average transaction-weighted rate of the preceding day. In practice, the official and market rates have never differed by more than 2%. (Country Report No. 12/329)
Malawi	The IMF staff report for the First Review under the Extended Credit Facility Arrangement with Malawi states as of December 6, 2012, the IMF staff is in the process of reviewing recent reforms to make an assessment of Malawi's exchange rate system. (Country Report No. 13/119)
Maldives	The IMF staff report for the 2010 Article IV consultation with Maldives states that, as of January 24, 2011, Maldives maintained an exchange restriction subject to IMF approval under Article VIII, Section 2(a), of the IMF's Articles of Agreement, arising from the Maldives Monetary Authority's policy of rationing its supply of foreign exchange to commercial banks. This rationing by a governmental agency has caused the channeling of foreign exchange transactions for current international transactions to the parallel market where transactions take place at an exchange rate that deviates by more than 2% from the official exchange rate. The more than 2% exchange rate spread gives rise to a multiple currency practice subject to IMF approval under Article VIII, Section 3, and also to an exchange restriction given the additional cost involved for obtaining foreign exchange. (Country Report No. 11/293)

Table 9 (continued)

Country[1]	Exchange Restrictions and/or Multiple Currency Practices[2]
Mongolia	The IMF staff report for the 2012 Article IV Consultation and Third Post-Program Monitoring states that, as of November 1, 2012, Mongolia maintained two multiple currency practices (MCPs) subject to IMF jurisdiction. First, the modalities of the multiprice auction system give rise to an MCP since there is no mechanism in place that ensures that exchange rates of accepted bids at the multiprice auction do not deviate by more than 2%. In addition, Mongolia has an official exchange rate (reference rate) that is mandatorily used for government transactions (as opposed to the commercial market rate). Therefore, by way of official action, the authorities have created market segmentation. While Order #699 of the Bank of Mongolia issued December 3, 2010, sets forth that the reference rate is determined based on the weighted average of market rates used from 4:00 p.m. of the previous day to 4:00 p.m. of the current day, the IMF staff is of the view that this order does not eliminate the market segmentation and multiplicity of effective rates arising from it. Accordingly, in the absence of a mechanism to ensure that the commercial rates and the reference rate do not deviate by more than 2%, the way the reference rate is used in government transaction gives rise to an MCP subject to IMF approval. (Country Report No. 12/320)
Montenegro	The IMF staff report for the 2012 Article IV consultation with the Republic of Montenegro states that, as of April 30, 2012, Montenegro maintained an exchange system free of restrictions on the making of payments and transfers for current international transactions, except with respect to pre-1992 blocked foreign currency savings accounts. (Country Report No. 12/122)
Myanmar	The IMF staff report for the 2011 Article IV consultation with Myanmar states that, as of March 5, 2012, Myanmar maintained exchange restrictions and multiple currency practices subject to IMF approval under Article VIII. Exchange restrictions subject to IMF jurisdiction arise from (1) advance import deposit requirements; (2) 100% margin requirements; (3) general restrictions on the availability and use of foreign exchange as such; (4) general restrictions on the making of payments and transfers related to invisibles; (5) the extra burden caused by official action imposing additional costs for exchange transactions; (6) official action that gives rise to multiple effective exchange rates in the markets (as well as potential deviations absent a mechanism to prevent spreads) with respect to the official exchange rate compared with all other exchange rates, the foreign exchange certificates (FEC) rate, and the "Thein Phyu counter rate" (TP rate); and (7) broken cross-rates. (Country Report No. 12/104)
Nepal	The IMF staff report for the 2012 Article IV consultation with Nepal states that as of November 2, 2012, Nepal maintained an exchange restriction under Article VIII, arising due to the limit of 75% placed by the Industrial Enterprise Act on conversion and transfer to foreign currency of salaries on nonresidents from countries where convertible currencies circulate. (Country Report No. 12/326)
Nigeria	The IMF staff report for the 2011 Article IV consultation with Nigeria states that, as of February 9, 2012, multiple prices are a technical characteristic of the CB's Dutch auction system and can give rise to multiple currency practices (MCPs). The IMF staff is currently conducting a comprehensive review of Nigeria's exchange system to identify the extent of any further restrictions and MCPs subject to IMF approval. (Country Report No. 12/194)
São Tomé and Príncipe	The IMF staff report for the First Review under the Three-Year Arrangement with São Tomé and Príncipe states that as of July 6, 2012, São Tomé and Príncipe maintained one measure subject to IMF approval under Article VIII: an exchange restriction arising from Article 3(i) and Article 10.1(b) of the Investment Code (Law No. 7/2008) regarding limitations on the transferability of net income from investment. The restriction results from the requirement that taxes and other obligations to the government have to be paid/fulfilled as a condition for transfer, to the extent the requirement includes the payment of taxes and the fulfillment of obligations unrelated to the net income to be transferred. (Country Report No. 12/216)
Serbia	The IMF staff report on the 2010 Article IV Consultation and Third Review under the Stand-By Arrangement and Financing Assurances states that, as of March 18, 2010, Serbia maintained a floating exchange rate system free of restrictions on current international payments and transfers, except with respect to blocked pre-1991 foreign currency savings accounts. (Country Report No. 10/93)
Sierra Leone	The IMF staff report for the Fourth Review under the Three-Year Arrangement under Extended Credit Facility states that, as of September 5, 2012, Sierra Leone maintained one multiple currency practice subject to IMF jurisdiction arising from the applied multiple- price Dutch auction system, as there is no formal mechanism in place to prevent spreads of effective rates between winning bids from exceeding 2% percent. (Country Report No. 12/285)

Table 9 (concluded)

Country[1]	Exchange Restrictions and/or Multiple Currency Practices[2]
Sudan	The IMF staff report for the 2012 Article IV Consultation with Sudan states that as of September 7, 2012, Sudan maintained (1) an exchange restriction and a multiple currency practice arising from the imposition by the government of a cash margin requirement for most imports and (2) an exchange restriction arising from the imposition of an absolute ceiling on foreign exchange for travel, subject to IMF approval under Article VIII, Sections 2(a) and 3. In addition, Sudan recently introduced additional exchange measures, and the IMF staff is currently assessing these measures to determine their compliance with Article VIII. (Country Report No. 12/298)
Suriname	The IMF staff report for the 2012 Article IV consultation with Suriname states that, as of July 17, 2012, Suriname maintained multiple currency practices arising from the spread of more than 2% between the buying and the selling rates in the official market for government transactions and also from the possible spread of more than 2% between these official rates for government transactions and those in the commercial markets that can take place within the established band. (Country Report No. 12/281)
Swaziland	The IMF staff report for the 2011 Article IV consultation with Swaziland states that, as of December 30, 2011, Swaziland maintained one exchange restriction subject to IMF approval under Article VIII. This arises from a 50% limit on the provision for advance payments for the import of certain capital goods. (Country Report No. 12/37)
Syria	The IMF staff report for the 2009 Article IV Consultation with Syria states that, as of February 12, 2010, Syria continued to maintain, under Article XIV, restrictions on payments and transfers for current international transactions, including administrative allocation of foreign exchange. Syria also maintained exchange measures that are subject to IMF approval under Article VIII: (1) prohibition against purchases by private parties of foreign exchange from the banking system for some current international transactions; (2) a multiple currency practice resulting from divergences of more than 2% between the official exchange rate and officially recognized market exchange rates; (3) a non-interest-bearing advance import deposit requirement of 75–100% for public sector imports; and (4) an exchange restriction arising from the net debt under inoperative bilateral payments arrangements with the Islamic Republic of Iran and Sri Lanka. (Country Report No. 10/86)
Tunisia	The IMF staff report for the 2012 Article IV consultation with Tunisia states that, as of July 10, 2012, Tunisia maintained a multiple currency practice resulting from honoring exchange rate guarantees extended prior to August 1988 to development banks, which will automatically expire after maturity of existing commitments (total loans covered by these guarantees amount to about US$20 million). (Country Report No. 12/255)
Ukraine	The IMF staff report for the 2012 Article IV Consultations with Ukraine states that as of June 18, 2012, Ukraine maintained multiple currency practices arising from (1) the use of the official exchange rate for certain government transactions, and (2) the requirement that a Ukrainian resident who sells previously purchased foreign exchange not used within 10 days (including foreign exchange returned to the resident because the counterparty failed to fulfill its obligations under an import contract) transfer 100% of the positive difference from the sale price, on a quarterly basis, to the state budget. (Country Report No. 12/315)
Zambia	The IMF staff report for the 2012 Article IV Consultations with Zambia states that, as of May 25, 2012, Zambia maintained an exchange restriction shown by the accumulation of external payments arrears, which is subject to IMF approval under Article VIII. (Country Report No. 12/200)
Zimbabwe	The IMF staff report for the 2012 Article IV consultation with Zimbabwe states that, as of September 10, 2012, apart from one remaining exchange restriction subject to IMF jurisdiction arising from unsettled balances under an inoperative bilateral payments agreement with Malaysia, payments and transfers for current international transactions can now be effected without restriction. (Country Report No. 12/279)

Source: IMF staff reports.

[1] Includes 188 member countries and three territories: Aruba, Curacao and Sint Maarten (all Netherlands) and Hong Kong SAR (China).

[2] The measures described in this table are quoted from IMF staff reports issued as of December 31, 2012, and may have changed subsequently to the date when they were reported. The table does not include countries maintaining exchange restrictions or multiple currency practices whose IMF staff reports are unpublished unless the authorities have consented to publication.

Regulatory Framework for Foreign Exchange Transactions

This section surveys the measures reported by members with respect to the regulatory framework for foreign exchange transactions for the period January 2012 to August 2013. This section is divided into five major categories: trade-related measures, current invisible transactions and transfers, account transactions, capital controls, and provisions specific to commercial banks and institutional investors.

Trade-Related Measures

Trade-related measures were predominantly easing measures, continuing a trend observed in recent years despite a weak recovery in the world economy. The total number of measures (adjusted for a factor explained below) amounted to 145, of which 76 were easing, 52 tightening, and 17 neutral.

Imports and import payments

The number of measures relating to imports and import payments (see adjustment in footnote below) amounted to 100, of which 50 were easing measures, 36 were tightening measures, and 14 were neutral measures.[20] With respect to easing measures, several members liberalized advance payments for imports. For example, Belarus eliminated the requirement of central bank permission for advance import payments from foreign currency proceeds received by residents through transactions other than bank loans. China eliminated requirements for advance payments. Fiji increased the limit on advance payments for imports. Moldova extended the period for imports of goods and services to be realized from one year to two years from the date of advance payments. Myanmar eliminated a 100 percent advance payment requirement. South Africa and Swaziland raised the amount of advance payments that may be made for imports up to R 10 million from 50 percent to 100 percent of ex-factory cost.

Some members liberalized other aspects of their import and payment regimes. For example, Bulgaria eliminated the import licensing requirement for certain grains, roots, and tubers and raised the threshold over which payments and transfers require documentation. Bangladesh permitted a markup over the London interbank offered rate for imports on usance terms and permitted importers to obtain buyer credits from abroad for a period not exceeding one year. Fiji increased the amount that authorized dealers may approve for merchandise imports. Maldives expanded the list of products subject to zero duty. Mexico reduced duties for a number of tariff lines and reduced the duty to zero for certain products destined for consumption in border areas. Myanmar revoked the foreign exchange balancing requirement that linked import payments to export earnings. EU countries eliminated limits on imports of steel from Russia on its accession to the World Trade Organization. Malawi discontinued verification of import documents for imports valued below a threshold. Lifting a ban of several years, the United States allowed the importation of most goods from Myanmar.

The scope for free trade agreements continued to expand. The ASEAN-Australia–New Zealand Free Trade Agreement (AANZFTA) went into effect with Indonesia. A free trade agreement between Panama and the United States went into effect. Venezuela became a member of MERCOSUR.

With respect to tightening measures, several members raised import duties, banned certain items, or introduced general import licensing. In compliance with MERCOSUR commitments, Argentina raised the duty on 100 tariff items imported from out of zone. Denmark required import licenses for certain wood products from Russia. In the face of heavy balance-of-payments pressures, Egypt issued an import priority list for the allocation of foreign exchange by banks. Malaysia adopted a negative import list. Micronesia and Moldova raised the duty on cigarettes and on liquefied natural gas, respectively. Moldova also raised excise taxes on liquefied petroleum gas. Kuwait issued bans, often source-specific, on beef, poultry, derived products, and

---

[20] During the period under review, Kuwait imposed 26 highly detailed, mainly source-specific, bans on imports of beef, poultry, derived meat products, live animals, and certain olive oil, while lifting 8 bans. Including these measures raises the number of reported import and import payment measures to 134, with 59 easing measures and 62 tightening measures. The implication of slightly more tightening than easing in this unadjusted count derives from the degree of detail in Kuwait's measures.

live animals and banned the importation of certain weapons, used tires, chewable tobacco, and cigarettes and other tobacco products unless the packaging contained a health warning on the front. Portugal and the United States banned charcoal imports from Somalia, and Iraq imposed licensing requirements for imports.

Import regimes were tightened in various other ways. To promote the use of letters of credit in import payments, Iraq sells foreign exchange for import letters of credit at a rate determined by adding ID 9 per U.S. dollar to the auction rate while adding ID 13 for other import payments. Kazakhstan required banks to monitor the return of unused portions of an import advance in resident importers' accounts. Mauritania required a minimum deposit of 10 percent on documentary credits for essential imports, 20 percent for hydrocarbon imports, and 40 percent for other products. In response to balance of payments pressures, Sri Lanka imposed a 100 percent margin deposit requirement against letters of credit for imports of certain goods, and Ukraine reduced the deadline for receipt of imported goods and services from 180 days to 90 days from the date of payment.

Exports and export proceeds

During this reporting period, there were substantially more easing measures than tightening measures. Of the 45 measures reported, 26 were easing, 16 tightening, and 3 neutral.

With respect to easing measures, some members liberalized the deadline for the repatriation of export proceeds and the fraction that must be converted to local currency. For example, Argentina extended the period from the date of the bill of lading for deposit of the proceeds of exports to affiliates from 15 to 30 days. To provide immediate access to proceeds for exporters, Bangladesh permitted export bills to be discounted by authorized dealers. Bhutan lengthened the period for the repatriation of export proceeds from India to 90 days. As part of the continued liberalization of the exchange regime, Moldova extended the deadline for repatriation of proceeds from one to two years. Malawi reduced the percentage of export proceeds that must be converted to local currency on receipt from 40 to 20 percent.

Some members also liberalized verification and means of repatriation. Following years of continued easing of the export surrender requirement, China revoked the export proceeds verification system. Kazakhstan eliminated the use of a transaction passport with which banks for several years monitored the repatriation of export proceeds. Although Indonesia required receipt of export proceeds through the traditional banking system, such receipts may subsequently be freely transferred abroad. Serbia permitted receipt of proceeds from electronic sales of goods through e-money institutions.

Exports were also promoted through agreements. The Canada-Panama Free Trade Agreement went into effect in 2013. Kosovo began to benefit from a preferential agreement with the European Union that will last until 2015.

Among miscellaneous easing measures, Bolivia authorized exports of sugar if domestic supplies at a fair price are adequate. Myanmar revoked the commercial tax on exports, with some exceptions. In line with global easing of restrictions against Myanmar, Canada removed Myanmar from its Area Control List.

A few members tightened the regulations on repatriation and surrender of export proceeds. Argentina required the surrender of export proceeds, advance payments, and prefinancing within 15 days of disbursement. After extending the deadline for the repatriation of export proceeds from 6 to 12 months in late 2012, India shortened the deadline to 9 months in early 2013. Sudan required the repatriation of export proceeds under sight letters of credit and cash against documents within one month of shipment. Ukraine reduced the deadline for repatriation of proceeds from 180 to 90 days.

Current Invisible Transactions and Current Transfers

This section discusses nontrade payments and transfers that are included in the current account of the balance of payments. Under this category are income from investment (for example, profits, dividends, interest); payments for travel, education expenses, medical expenses, subscription or membership fees; and unrequited transfers (for example, remittance of nonresidents' salaries and wages). The tendency toward substantial easing of measures in this category has continued. In the period under review, the relevant measures totaled 70, of which 45, 22, and 3 were easing, tightening, and neutral measures, respectively. This compares with 45 measures in the previous reporting period, of which 33 were easing measures and 11 were tightening measures.

Payments for current invisibles and current transfers

Out of 60 measures relating to payments for current invisibles, 38 were easing measures and 20 were tightening measures. On measures in the easing direction, for example, Bangladesh, Mauritania, and Myanmar raised travel allowances. Bangladesh authorized payment without approval of commissions to foreign stock brokerage firms for services to foreign investors with respect to investment in Bangladesh and increased the limit on payments by information technology firms for business purposes. Bhutan permitted citizens traveling to India for medical treatment to purchase foreign exchange cash up to a limit and to transmit the remainder by direct transfer to the hospital's account. Much as for import payments, Bulgaria required documentation for payments and transfers for invisibles above a certain limit, and Fiji and India increased the threshold above which documentation is required for payments. Fiji eased the limits on payments and transfers for airline ticket sales, medical treatment, trade-related payments, and remittances for miscellaneous purposes without documentation. In addition, Fiji delegated approval of transfers to authorized banks of profits and dividends, up to a limit. Iraq eliminated the tax clearance requirement for transfers of foreign exchange purchased at auction. Bangladesh permitted resident foreign nationals to make monthly remittances out of their current savings up to 75 percent of their net income to cover their commitments abroad. Morocco eased the transfer of savings on income by eliminating the obligation to deduct expenditures incurred in Morocco. Myanmar liberalized remittances of salaries, compensation payments for accidents, pension payments, income of foreign airlines, and air freight charges. Sudan authorized local banks to process transfers and current payments for banks operating in the free zone.

In the tightening direction, several examples may be cited. To stem capital flight, Argentina set new requirements for purchases of banknotes or foreign exchange for travel, gifts, and educational expenses and reduced the time by which advance payment of interest on foreign loans may be made from 15 to 5 days before the due date. It also required approval for payments for professional and technical services, patents, trademarks, and commissions in transactions between related entities or if the beneficiary resides or the account is located in a tax haven. Australia required approval for payments above a threshold in high-risk transactions, including those in which one party is an individual in the Islamic Republic of Iran or a legal entity incorporated there. Bhutan limited personal travel allowances according to a daily amount and a cumulative monthly amount, while Iran reduced in two successive steps the amount of foreign exchange that may be purchased for travel. Ecuador increased the rate of the exchange tax on transfers abroad. Iraq reduced the amount of foreign exchange that may be bought for any purpose on proof of identity with a passport only, and Ukraine tightened procedures for identifying persons in foreign exchange transactions. In the midst of a financial crisis, in March 2013, Cyprus imposed limits (with larger amounts requiring approval) on payments for educational allowances, transfers for normal business activity, and banknotes taken for travel abroad. Payments through credit and debit cards were also subject to limits. In subsequent weeks, Cyprus began easing the above-mentioned limits and removed the limit on payments by credit or debit cards.

Proceeds from current invisibles and current transfers

The few measures relating to proceeds from invisible transactions were mainly easing measures (7 of 10). For example, Bangladesh permitted up to 50 percent of repatriated foreign exchange to be credited against payments for business process outsourcing, raised the threshold above which inward remittances must be declared, and raised the maximum amount of proceeds from small-value services that may be received through online payment service providers. In line with the measures implemented on export proceeds, Malawi lowered the percentage of proceeds that must be converted to local currency on receipt, and Moldova extended the deadline for repatriating proceeds from one to two years.

In contrast, with respect to tightening measures, Argentina required proceeds to be credited to a demand account in a local financial institution. For a period of six months, Ukraine required transfers in Group 1 foreign exchange and Russian rubles that exceed a certain threshold to be converted to local currency to stem depreciation pressure on the currency.

Account Transactions

Members reported 95 changes in regulations on resident and nonresident accounts, of which 65 were easing measures, 24 were tightening measures, and 6 were neutral measures. Despite the overall easing trend, some members have tightened regulations on account transactions in response to acute financial crises.

Resident Accounts

Changes referring to resident accounts numbered 55, of which 37 were easing measures, 14 were tightening measures, and 4 were neutral measures. Easing measures refer to the opening of resident accounts, eligible credits, and withdrawals. For example, Bhutan permitted nongovernmental organizations and foreign exchange earners to open U.S. dollar–denominated accounts with local banks. It also allowed local industries to retain 10 percent of their Indian rupee earnings in rupee accounts with local banks. In Morocco, entities belonging to a finance city consortium were authorized to open foreign currency or convertible dirham accounts, and Sudan permitted local contractors to open foreign currency accounts. Pakistan permitted authorized dealers to use foreign currency accounts to extend trade loans in foreign currency. India allowed exporters to credit earnings in foreign currency to their foreign currency accounts but required the balance to be converted to rupees by the end of the subsequent month. Burundi revoked limits on withdrawals from resident foreign currency accounts. Colombia permitted residents to transfer funds to and from clearing accounts of the same account holder. Myanmar permitted withdrawals in cash up to US$10,000. Sri Lanka eased the transfers of funds between nonresident and resident foreign currency accounts.

Fewer members implemented tightening measures. As for withdrawals, Argentina required that withdrawal of foreign currency from ATMs abroad be debited only against foreign currency accounts held locally. To control possible outflows from domestic estates, Iceland rescinded the exemption from capital controls of payments from bankruptcy and from contractual claims in accordance with the composition of creditors' agreements. Iran prohibited the purchase of foreign currency exceeding a certain amount for the purpose of opening a foreign currency account. Tunisia required surplus funds in foreign currency accounts to be converted to dinars. In March 2013, reflecting an ongoing financial crisis, Cyprus prohibited the cashing of checks, limited daily withdrawals in cash to €300, and prohibited the establishment of new accounts unless funded by transfers from abroad. At the same time, Cyprus imposed limits on noncash transfers from one bank to another bank in Cyprus and transfers abroad. Subsequently, these restrictions were eased gradually: the limit on cash withdrawals was raised to €500 for legal persons; limits on noncash payments to another bank in Cyprus were increased; transfers of term deposits were permitted within the same institution and for purchases of real estate; and new bank accounts were authorized if the accounts were funded with cash for new term deposits of at least three months or for the servicing of new loans.

Nonresident Accounts

Of the 44 measures reported for nonresident accounts, 32 were easing measures (many of which also refer to measures taken by Cyprus in the context of the gradual easing of the restrictions imposed in late March— because they applied equally to resident and nonresident accounts), 10 were tightening measures, and 2 were neutral measures. With respect to easing measures, Bhutan permitted nonresidents to withdraw a specific amount in cash and the balance through other payment instruments on the closure of their accounts. Honduras authorized financial institutions to accept deposits in Canadian dollars. India permitted the transfer of funds from nonresident ordinary accounts to nonresident external accounts within an overall ceiling, while Sri Lanka permitted transfers between foreign currency accounts of nonresidents and residents. Myanmar allowed nonresidents to maintain accounts with public and private banks. Libya permitted nonresident Libyans to open accounts in convertible dinars and foreign currency.

With respect to tightening measures, Bhutan revoked permission for nonresidents to maintain domestic currency accounts in Bhutan. Croatia revoked a specific regulation governing nonresident bank accounts. Ukraine prohibited deposits of foreign exchange cash in investment accounts of foreign investors.

Capital Controls

There was a continuation of the overall trend toward the liberalization of capital transactions in the midst of slow global recovery and an increase in the volatility of capital flows. As a result, while some countries continued their gradual liberalization, others instituted capital controls in response to the increased volatility and the changing global environment. Capital flows to emerging markets, which recovered after the onset of the global financial crisis but stayed slightly below precrisis peaks, ended in 2011 because of concern about growing European debt. Capital flows were generally weak during most of 2012, but international investors returned to emerging markets in the last quarter of 2012 in search of yield, partly in response to measures taken in Europe (the European Central Bank's Outright Monetary Transactions program) and in the United States (the Federal Reserve's third quantitative easing program). Volatility increased during the early part of 2013 as flows began shifting to advanced economies because of improved U.S. growth prospects, new pro-growth policies in Japan, weaker growth prospects in emerging markets, and fears about early tapering of U.S. monetary stimulus. In response, some emerging markets rolled back controls to ease conditions for inflows.

Easing measures dominated for both inflows and outflows, despite an increase in the overall number of measures reported over last year. Between January 1, 2012, and August 31, 2013, IMF members reported 202 measures compared with 164 measures during the previous period (January 2011 to July 2012). The increase in the aggregate number of measures reported reflects a large number of changes implemented in Cyprus.[21] Of the total, 133 (or about 66 percent) of the measures implemented were directed toward easing capital flows. (During the previous year, it was about 60 percent.) Of the remaining measures, 57 (or about 28 percent) were tightening measures and the rest (about 6 percent) were neutral.

The measures included in this section are also considered to be capital flow management measures (CFMs) as defined by the IMF's institutional view on the liberalization and management of capital flows.[22] In addition to capital controls included in this section, prudential-type measures discussed in the next section may also be CFMs if they were designed to influence capital flows. However, the AREAER does not use this terminology because classifying a measure as a CFM requires substantial background information and considerable judgment, which is beyond the scope of the analysis conducted for building the AREAER database.

---

[21] Cyprus, to deal with its economic crisis, imposed wide-ranging restrictions in March 2013 that significantly constrained capital transactions across many categories. Subsequently, as conditions improved, restrictions were gradually eased in several steps starting as early as April 2013. The AREAER records the imposition of these restrictions and their step-by-step removal across many categories of transactions, thereby showing a large number of measures taken by Cyprus.

[22] CFMs encompass a broad spectrum of measures. For the purposes of the IMF's institutional view, the term "capital flow management measures" refers to measures designed to limit capital flows. CFMs comprise residency-based CFMs, which encompass a variety of measures (including taxes and regulations) affecting cross-border financial activity that discriminate on the basis of residency—also generally referred to as capital controls—and other CFMs, which do not discriminate on the basis of residency, but are nonetheless designed to limit capital flows. These other CFMs typically include measures, such as some prudential measures, that differentiate transactions on the basis of currency as well as other measures that typically apply to the nonfinancial sector. The concept of capital controls in the AREAER is quite similar to that of the CFM: it encompasses regulations that limit capital flows and includes various measures that regulate the conclusion or execution of transactions and transfers and the holding of assets at home by nonresidents and abroad by residents. See "The Liberalization and Management of Capital Flows: An Institutional View." www.imf.org/external/np/pp/eng/2012/111412.pdf.

Repatriation and surrender requirements

Only a few countries modified repatriation and surrender requirements with respect to capital transactions. All the measures related to some form of tightening. Argentina reduced to 30 days the repatriation period for settlement of proceeds related to financial debts and issuance of securities abroad. Indonesia now requires that proceeds from issuance of loans abroad be received through domestic banks, though without an obligation to keep the funds in such banks or to convert them to domestic currency.

Controls on capital and money market instruments

The total number of measures taken (39) to adjust controls on capital and money market instruments was less than the number of measures taken last year. Measures to ease (22) as opposed to tighten (13) controls on capital and money market instruments were aimed at easing outflows more than inflows, unlike last year, when the bulk of the measures was directed at easing inflows.

The measures to ease inflows included increased access to the domestic securities market, greater equity participation by foreigners, and relaxation of conditions for residents to receive proceeds of sales of foreign securities and debt instruments. China expanded the qualified foreign investors program by permitting Hong Kong subsidiaries of Chinese banks, insurers, and financial institutions to invest in domestic securities markets using renminbi proceeds raised in Hong Kong SAR. Brazil lowered the financial operations tax (imposto sobre operações financeiras—IOF) rate related to inflows from cancellation of depository receipts invested in the acquisition of stock on the stock market. India permitted qualified investors to buy eligible corporate debt instruments and eased and simplified investment limits for foreign institutional investors' purchases of government securities. Serbia allowed residents who own certain foreign securities to receive proceeds from their sale. Thailand increased the scope of foreign equity participation in securities and asset management companies. Bangladesh eliminated the one-year holding period for nonresident investors buying government bonds.

Measures to tighten inflows covered resident institutions issuing shares abroad and nonresidents issuing shares in the domestic market. Sudan barred domestic banks from issuing shares overseas without approval, and Turkey replaced a registration system with an approval requirement for nonresidents making a public offering. Uruguay imposed a reserve requirement on nonresidents holding a position in central bank or government securities denominated in local currency or inflation index units.

Tightening measures on outflows included measures to ease pressure on the domestic exchange market and prevent capital flight. For example, Argentina tightened controls to safeguard reserves by limiting the use by financial institutions of their overall foreign exchange position for transactions in the secondary market and required residents to obtain central bank approval to access the local foreign exchange market for the purchase of external assets not earmarked for a specific purpose. Cyprus imposed limits on the transfer of funds overseas by individuals and for normal business activity; transfers of amounts above the limit require approval. Iceland prohibited the purchase of foreign currency for payment of bond principal. Ecuador increased the tax on transfers abroad. Bolivia reduced the ceiling for insurance companies' investments abroad.

Easing outflow measures relaxed conditions on portfolio investment abroad by residents. Cyprus gradually reversed some of the controls imposed on outward transfers. In particular, it increased, in phases, the limits on depositors' automatic transfers abroad for normal business activity. India eased conditions for the acquisition by residents of shares in foreign companies where they work or for which they have provided professional services. Fiji relaxed the limit on investment overseas by individuals and permitted commercial banks to open foreign currency accounts to facilitate such investments overseas. Thailand permitted companies listed on the local stock exchange to invest without limit in securities issued abroad by Thai juridical persons and up to US$50 million an investor in foreign securities without central bank approval. Turkey permitted collective investment funds to invest up to 10 percent of their portfolio value in stock exchange mutual fund units traded on foreign exchanges.

Controls on derivatives and other instruments

There was a somewhat greater trend toward easing for such transactions (14 of 20), unlike last year, when the measures were almost equally divided between easing and tightening. An equally small number of countries reported changes this reporting period as in the past period, although the total number of measures reported was greater compared with last year, mostly because of Cyprus. About half the easing measures applied to both outflows and inflows.

The restrictions on outflows in Cyprus imposed limitations on derivative transactions too. However, these are temporary measures, and their gradual easing would allow such transactions to resume. Easing measures in Malaysia allowed nonbank nonresidents to engage in ringgit-denominated interest rate derivative contracts with domestic banks with or without a firm underlying commitment and domestic banks to settle such derivative contracts with nonbank nonresidents in ringgit or foreign currency. Other easing measures affected both inflows and outflows. Argentina allowed authorized dealers to engage in arbitrage and swaps with foreign financial entities. El Salvador allowed banks to undertake forward foreign exchange contracts. Lebanon expanded the number of nonresident counterparties with which financial intermediaries could enter into derivative contracts on their own behalf or on behalf of clients. Paraguay permitted nonresident agents to purchase and sell foreign exchange forward contracts. Nonresidents and qualifying South African and Common Monetary Area entities may now engage in Zambian-referenced grain derivative contracts, which may be listed on the South African stock exchange. Sri Lanka, which tightened regulation on the period of maturity of forward foreign exchange contracts by imposing a 90-day limit in early 2012, eliminated it in early 2013.

Controls on credit operations

Controls on cross-border lending were mostly eased, with about 70 percent of measures aimed at relaxing conditions. The trend was more pronounced than last year. The total number of measures virtually doubled compared with last year. In addition, whereas last year such measures were the second most common, following measures related to controls on capital and money market instruments, this year, they were overall the most frequent type of measures implemented. Of the easing measures, about 64 percent were targeted at inflows. The majority of tightening measures targeted outflows.

Inflow easing measures were mostly related to external borrowing. Against a backdrop of declining capital flows, Brazil decreased the maturity of external loans in late 2012 subject to the IOF tax, exempting those with a maturity longer than one year from the tax in order to attract inflows. Earlier in the year, it had increased the maximum maturity subject to the IOF tax to five years to manage inflows. More than half the measures toward easing inflows were reported by India as it continued its liberalization of the external commercial borrowing (ECB) regime. Measures by India to ease ECB conditions include expanded access limits to existing users (for example, power sector, infrastructure companies) and access to ECB for new users (for example, for civil aviation; maintenance of toll systems; developers of the National Manufacturing Investment Zone; Small Industries Development Bank of India for micro, small, and medium enterprises; affordable housing projects). Serbia also continued liberalizing external borrowing to attract inflows and as part of its gradual liberalization of capital flows. It eliminated the reserve balance requirement on credit and foreign borrowing by leasing companies; branches of foreign legal entities were allowed to borrow from nonresident founders at maturities longer than one year; natural persons were allowed to borrow abroad at maturities longer than one year; short-term financial loans from abroad with maturities of more than three months for export financing were expanded beyond agricultural loans; banks were permitted to access short-term financial loans from abroad; and resident natural persons were allowed to obtain long-term cross-border financial loans for purposes other than imports of goods and services. Sri Lanka introduced a special borrowing program for domestic companies to allow them to borrow up to US$10 million a year and up toUS$30 million for a period of three years through December 31, 2015; larger amounts remain subject to approval. Sri Lanka also eliminated a ceiling on banks' credit growth funded with external borrowing and exempted foreign borrowing of commercial banks up to US$50 million each from regulatory limits for three years through December 31, 2015.

Outflow easing measures generally tended to relax the conditions on extending loans to nonresidents and on repaying external loans. India eased conditions on the repayment of loans to nonresidents by allowing payment to nonresidents' foreign currency accounts. Fiji increased the maximum on repayment of principal and interest. Lebanon eliminated the limit based on tier 1 capital on total loans extended in countries rated

BBB or higher. Serbia eliminated the requirement that loans between a resident legal person and its subsidiary abroad be financed from profit realized abroad. Tunisia allowed resident banks to access the local foreign exchange market to fund loans to nonresident service companies engaged in imports and exports and to nonresident international trading companies engaged in exports of local products. Vietnam permitted domestic banks to provide guarantees to nonresident borrowers. Bangladesh permitted importers to obtain buyer's credit from abroad for a period not exceeding one year and at an interest cost not exceeding 6 percent a year.

Tightening measures were mostly related to outflows. Argentina took steps to ease potential pressure on the foreign exchange market and safeguard reserves by limiting the use of the local foreign exchange market to access funds related to external loans. For instance, it imposed conditions for repaying external debt if the local foreign exchange market was accessed for funds and required customers receiving foreign currency loans from domestic financial institutions to surrender the funds in the local foreign exchange market. Cyprus imposed measures to safeguard financial stability by limiting deposit withdrawals and started relaxing them shortly thereafter to protect economic activity. Iceland rescinded exemptions from capital control on payments from bankruptcy and resolution and bank winding-up committees to reduce potential pressure in the foreign exchange market. Lebanon prohibited banks and financial institutions from performing treasury placements abroad other than for operating accounts, except with correspondents rated at least BBB. Lebanon also imposed limits on credit used abroad: credit extended by a domestic bank and its branches abroad to a single borrower (or group of related borrowers) and used abroad may not exceed 10 percent of tier 1 capital, and total credit granted to a domestic bank and its foreign branches for use abroad may not exceed four times tier 1 capital. In response to deteriorating foreign exchange market conditions, Ukraine reduced the term for which residents may extend commercial credit to nonresidents from 180 days to 90 days for six months.

Very few inflow tightening measures were imposed. Colombia barred residents from obtaining foreign currency loans from nonresident individuals. To reduce the pace of domestic credit growth, Sri Lanka imposed a temporary limit on credit growth, limiting the amount of funding from abroad that could be channeled into local lending in early 2012, but lifted the measure in less than a year.

Controls on direct investment

The liberalization trend continued to be most pronounced in foreign direct investment. Easing measures far outweighed tightening measures, similarly to last year. The number of measures implemented to ease inflows was lower than those targeted at easing outflows. The total number of measures was slightly higher than last year.

Inflow easing measures included those that raised automatic threshold levels, broadened the permissible sectors, and increased the level of equity participation. Australia, Mexico, and New Zealand increased the threshold below which investments are automatically permitted. Russia permitted certain types of investors to invest in strategic sectors. South Africa eased some of its rules governing the International Headquarter Company regime, including the approval requirement for direct investment; reduced the shareholding requirement to 10 percent; and permitted companies established under this regime to list shares and debt on the local stock exchange. South Africa also permitted companies listed on the local stock exchange to establish one subsidiary in South Africa for African and offshore operations that is not subject to foreign exchange restrictions. Thailand broadened the scope and amount of equity participation in the securities business to include forms of business other than brokerage. Turkey further liberalized the limit on foreign ownership in radio and television broadcasting.

With respect to outflow easing, Fiji further relaxed the limit on overseas investment by individuals and permitted such investment by nonbank financial institutions and companies with central bank approval. India eased conditions for the acquisition by residents of shares in foreign companies, and investment in Pakistan is now permitted. South Africa permitted limited outward investment in companies, branches, and offices outside the Common Monetary Area operating outside the investor's current line of business and allowed the transfer of additional capital overseas on approval. Morocco permitted bank accounts of domestic companies with foreign equity participation to be operated by nonresident foreign managers.

Only a handful of tightening measures were taken affecting outflows and inflows of direct investment. The measures imposed in Cyprus on transfers abroad also affected outward direct investment, but these were gradually eased. Malaysia tightened inflow controls by raising the minimum value of residential property foreigners may purchase. The Philippines tightened the registration requirement on all foreign direct investment. Argentina limited outflows by making central bank approval necessary for residents' purchases of external assets not earmarked for a specific purpose. South Africa imposed an approval requirement for treasury outsourcing companies before they may do business in the domestic foreign exchange market.

China eased the rules on transfers overseas of proceeds from liquidation of direct investment by eliminating the approval requirement. Fiji delegated the approval of withdrawal of investment, up to a limit, to authorized dealers from the central bank.

Controls on real estate transactions

There was no clear overall direction for measures affecting real estate transactions. Similarly to last year, almost as many measures were implemented to tighten and ease flows. Malaysia and Singapore took measures to stem inflows to residential property markets in an attempt to reduce the pressure on real estate prices. While Malaysia increased the minimum value of purchases, Singapore imposed additional stamp duty. In contrast, Turkey eased regulations on real estate acquisitions by foreign individuals, including by increasing the area a foreigner may acquire, and clarified rules on the acquisition of real estate by foreign companies. Outflows from real estate transactions were eased in China by eliminating the foreign currency approval procedures related to repatriation of proceeds from the sale of real estate by nonresidents. Korea liberalized overseas purchases of real estate by individuals for any purpose other than residence.

Controls on personal transactions

As in the previous reporting period, more measures were implemented to ease controls on personal transactions. However, given the relatively lower number of measures in this category, the easing trend reflects the gradual relaxation of controls initially imposed by Cyprus. Otherwise, the picture is more balanced between easing and tightening. Korea relaxed the notification requirement for won loans not exceeding 1 million won to residents from nonresidents. Serbia allowed borrowing by natural persons from abroad at maturities over a year and for purposes other than imports of goods and services. Colombia tightened requirements on residents' foreign currency loans by barring nonresident individuals from granting such loans. To ease pressure in the foreign exchange market, Ukraine required that foreign exchange transfers to resident individuals over a certain amount be converted to local currency. The measure is intended to remain in place for six months only. Outflows were eased by India as it relaxed conditions on the repayment of loans to nonresidents. Swaziland also eased outflows by increasing the amount individuals could invest abroad. In contrast, Argentina imposed restrictions on use of the local foreign exchange market to pay financial debts and required approval for the use of credit and debit cards that use international payment networks. Iraq reduced the amount of foreign exchange an individual may buy without documentation.

Provisions Specific to Commercial Banks and Institutional Investors

This section reviews developments in provisions specific to commercial banks and institutional investors, with a focus on prudential measures that are in the nature of capital controls.[23] The category Provisions specific to the financial sector covers monetary and prudential measures in addition to foreign exchange controls.[24] It includes, among other categories of financial institutions' transactions, borrowing abroad, lending to non-

---

[23] Capital controls and prudential measures are highly intertwined because of their overlapping application. For example, some prudential measures (for example, different reserve requirements for deposit accounts held by residents and nonresidents) could also be regarded as capital controls because they distinguish between transactions with residents and nonresidents and hence influence capital flows.

[24] Inclusion of an entry in this category does not necessarily indicate that the aim of the measure is to control the flow of capital.

residents, purchase of locally issued securities denominated in foreign exchange, and regulations pertaining to banks' and institutional investors' investments. These provisions may be similar or identical to the measures described in the respective categories of controls on accounts, capital and money market instruments, credit operations, and direct investments, if the same regulations apply to commercial banks and institutional investors as to other residents. In such cases, the measure also appears in the relevant category in the sections Capital Controls, Resident Accounts, and Nonresident Accounts.

Developments in 2012 and early 2013 were shaped by members' continued efforts to strengthen the financial regulatory framework, concerns about financial stability, and capital flow volatility. The developments mark two distinct trends compared with the previous reporting period: an increase in the number of capital control tightening measures and a shift toward the easing of prudential measures.

The number of reported changes in the financial sector regulatory framework exceeded the corresponding number in the previous period by 10 percent. The reported changes affected mainly banks and other financial institutions, with 17 percent of the measures introducing changes related to the regulatory framework of institutional investors. Although the majority of the 229 measures were of a prudential nature (70 percent), the increase in the number of changes consists mostly of changes in capital controls, with capital control tightening significantly increasing from the previous reporting period (by 18 measures). This tightening trend was more pronounced for commercial banks and other credit institutions than for institutional investors. Changes in the prudential regulations show a more balanced picture, with members implementing more easing measures than in the previous reporting period. Nonetheless, tightening changes dominate the measures implemented during January 2012–August 2013, except in the case of capital controls for institutional investors, for which measures easing capital controls slightly exceed tightening measures. The number of measures considered neutral increased only marginally from the previous reporting period, reflecting, among other things, continued work to revise and consolidate the current regulatory and institutional framework. The summary of the changes in this category is presented in Table 10.

Table 10. Provisions Specific to the Financial Sector, January 1, 2012–August 31, 2013

	Provisions Specific to Commercial Banks and Other Credit Institutions				Provisions Specific to Institutional Investors				Total
	Easing	Tightening	Neutral	Total	Easing	Tightening	Neutral	Total	
Capital Controls	11	34	1	46	11	10	0	21	67
Prudential Measures	42	70	31	143	4	5	10	19	162
Total	53	104	32	189	15	15	10	40	229

Source: AREAER database.

Commercial banks and other credit institutions

Changes in capital controls further tightened existing norms on commercial banks and other credit institutions (73 percent), suggesting that financial stability concerns in some countries may have required tools that were stronger than nondiscriminatory prudential measures. One of the most notable changes in this respect was the introduction of wide-ranging limitations on deposit withdrawals and cross-border transfers in Cyprus in March 2013, instituted to protect financial stability in the face of potentially destabilizing deposit outflows. Since then, restrictions have been gradually eased to reduce the impact on economic activity. Although caps on cash withdrawals and certain transfer limitations, in particular on large cross-border transactions, are still in place, restrictions on payments for regular business operations have been significantly eased. To protect the business service sector, the operations of foreign banks with international customers were exempted from the restrictions. Iceland also tightened capital controls first introduced in 2008 by removing an exemption to address potential balance-of-payments drains as a result of the winding-up of old bank estates.

Other measures to tighten capital controls included an increased tax on transfers abroad in Ecuador and on loans up to five years in Brazil in early 2012 (the latter was later reversed). To reduce reliance on more volatile short-term capital inflows, Brazil and Korea further tightened the limit on banks' derivative positions, and Latvia introduced a liquidity ratio that increases with the share of a bank's assets funded by nonresident deposits. Revised norms in Brazil require supervised entities to invest in certain foreign companies only as permanent investment and on approval by the Superintendence of Private Insurance. Capital controls were also tightened with respect to foreign exchange risk management (asymmetric open foreign exchange position limits) as discussed below.

The majority of the measures that ease controls involve cross-border loan transactions (Brazil, Pakistan, Serbia, Tunisia). For example, as it experienced diminishing pressure in the foreign exchange market from capital inflows, Brazil reduced the IOF rate on external borrowing with maturities longer than one year in the second half of 2012. To boost exports, banks may grant loans sourced in the foreign exchange market to nonresident service companies engaged in imports and exports in Tunisia and to nonresident international trading companies engaged in exports of products of local origin. The measures also reflect Cyprus's relaxation of previously introduced controls on external transfers by increasing the limits in several steps and removing the ceiling on payments with credit and debit cards abroad.

Other measures easing capital controls include changes in forward transactions in Fiji, where authorized banks were permitted to write net forward sales contracts up to F$20 million, and in Sri Lanka, where the 90-day limit on the maturity of forward foreign exchange contracts introduced in March 2012 was eliminated. Banks were authorized to accept funds in Canadian dollars in Honduras. Following a significant easing of controls on outward foreign direct investment in 2011, banks in South Africa were allowed to invest an additional 5 percent of their total liabilities, excluding total shareholder equity, for expansion in Africa.

The strengthening of the prudential framework of banks' operations started after the global financial crisis continued, albeit at a slower pace. Less than half of the reported measures that are not considered capital controls strengthened existing regulations. Some of the 70 changes implemented in the reporting period tightened regulations governing anti-money-laundering/combating the finance of terrorism (Argentina, Austria, San Marino); others aimed at reducing the risk of banking operations by adjusting regulatory limits and increasing liquidity buffers (Armenia, Lebanon, Poland, Serbia). Financial requirements for traders in over-the-counter derivatives were increased in Austria, and conditions on correspondent relations and limits on net credit exposure with correspondent banks abroad were tightened in Lebanon. A foreign exchange funding adequacy ratio to manage the maturity mismatch of banks' on-balance-sheet and off-balance-sheet foreign exchange positions was introduced in Hungary.[25] Reporting and disclosure requirements were tightened to increase transparency and boost confidence in the banking system in San Marino and Serbia and, as part of a broader reform of the financial sector regulatory framework, in Moldova. A stricter regime for the transfer of qualifying holdings in a bank's capital was introduced in Moldova, and the acquisition of qualified holdings in a bank or other financial organization headquartered outside Slovenia or the European Union became subject to Bank of Slovenia approval. In an effort to move away from crisis mode in the banking sector, San Marino introduced an extraordinary tax of 1.5 percent on the financial industry on the total amount of accumulated losses for entities that opted to carry forward tax losses incurred during 2009–12 without time limits.

While members continued to tighten the regulatory framework for banks and other credit institutions to reinforce financial stability, changes to ease regulatory constraints (42) have also increased compared with the previous reporting period (28). Reported changes easing banks' prudential framework were aimed mostly at supporting the restructuring and recovery of the banking sector and rolled back previous tightening in the aftermath of the global crisis.[26] For example, to facilitate the recovery of the banking sector, classification

---

[25] This ratio is obtained by dividing the sum of stable foreign exchange funds and net foreign exchange swap stock with maturities of more than one year by the outstanding weighted foreign-currency-denominated assets to be financed with maturities of more than one year.

[26] The number of easing changes is affected by the introduction of the reserve option mechanism in Turkey, under which a gradually increasing share of the required reserves on lira liabilities may be held in foreign currency and gold. The new regime was implemented in several steps (17) that increased the number of changes significantly. Discounting such changes, the number of easing changes remains slightly below the number of such changes last year.

rules for certain assets were eased in Moldova, San Marino, and Serbia. Guidelines for currency forwards were issued, enabling banks to engage in such operations in El Salvador. To boost credit growth, the loan-to-value limit on forint-denominated real-estate-backed mortgage loans was raised from 75 percent to 80 percent, and the loan-to-value limit on financial real estate leasing in forint was revoked in Hungary. India reduced the statutory liquidity ratio, and rules on banks' investments in legal entities exceeding 10 percent of the shares were relaxed in Kazakhstan. Several measures encouraged reorganization and concentration in the financial sector in San Marino, including tax benefits and credit facilities for banks to acquire the liabilities of entities under extraordinary administration and tax exemption on the transfers of assets, businesses, or business units in San Marino to affiliates.

There was continued modernization and harmonization of financial sector regulatory norms. Austria further updated its financial sector regulations related to the single euro payments area project, which aims to replace current national payment services with a common EU-wide payment service. Oversight of financial institutions' operations in Kazakhstan was transferred to the National Bank of the Republic of Kazakhstan. Kosovo significantly revised its financial sector regulatory framework, including norms on large exposures, credit risk management, and capital adequacy. Moldova and Romania amended financial sector regulations to ensure consistency between banking sector financial and prudential reporting. Poland introduced detailed rules on exposure concentration and large exposure limits. San Marino set up a deposit guarantee fund to enhance the stability of the banking system. A regulatory framework for microfinance organizations was introduced in Kazakhstan and Kosovo, and a new law for microfinance organizations was developed and submitted to Parliament in Moldova. The treatment of dormant accounts was harmonized in the West African Economic and Monetary Union countries.

Close to one-third of the reported changes in the regulatory framework for commercial banks and other credit institutions were related to reserve requirements, indicating the importance of reserve requirements in the pursuit of monetary policy and financial stability objectives and in the response to changes in capital flows. An almost equal number of easing and tightening changes were implemented in the reporting period.

- To create a macroprudential liquidity buffer in case of external shocks, Bolivia, Cambodia, Ghana, Haiti, Peru, Turkey, and Uruguay increased the rate of required reserves on local or foreign-currency-denominated liabilities.[27] Except for Croatia and India, all countries reporting changes in reserve requirements apply different reserve ratios to domestic and foreign currency liabilities. Bolivia introduced an additional reserve requirement on liabilities in foreign currency and units indexed to the U.S. dollar. With these changes, all deposits in foreign currency and units indexed to the U.S. dollar will be subject to a reserve requirement ranging from 45 percent to 66.5 percent by mid-2016. To address concerns with respect to consumer credit growth, the Central Bank of Tunisia imposed an additional 50 percent reserve requirement on increases in consumer credit in late 2012. The rate was subsequently reduced to 30 percent in March 2013, and plans were announced to remove the additional reserve requirements as soon as the quarterly rate of coverage reaches 110 percent.

- Reserve requirements were eased in Croatia, Egypt, India, Serbia, and Tajikistan by decreasing the rate of required reserves. To reduce dollarization, the reserve requirement on domestic currency deposits was reduced and set at the same rate as for foreign currency deposits in Angola. In contrast to the previous reporting period, when Russia set a higher reserve ratio on nonresidents' liabilities amid persistently high inflation expectations and with a view to preparing for an influx of capital, a single reserve requirement of 4.25 percent was set for all categories of liabilities subject to reserve requirements. Turkey allowed more choice in the denomination of the currency in which the reserve requirements must be met. Ghana moved to setting the reserve requirement of foreign exchange liabilities in local currency, and required reserves must increasingly be met in local currency in Serbia. Such a shift in the denomination of the required reserves usually also causes a one-time increase in the supply of foreign exchange in the foreign exchange market and may contribute to dedollarization.

---

[27] Depending on the policy objective, reserve requirement ratios are often differentiated according to maturity, the denomination of the liability, or the residency of the depositor/lender. (The latter are considered capital controls.)

As in the previous year, the framework for commercial banks' foreign exchange risk management was overwhelmingly tightened, likely reflecting concerns about the risks related to increased variability in the foreign exchange markets. Foreign exchange exposure limits, which are often imposed in an asymmetric manner, have been lowered in Egypt, Ghana, Kosovo, Rwanda, Sri Lanka, Tanzania, Vietnam, Zambia, and Zimbabwe with a view to reducing banks' foreign exchange risk and their ability to take a position against the currency.[28] In certain cases, the limits were reduced below 10 percent of capital. For example, the net open foreign exchange position limit was reduced to ±7.5 percent from ±20 percent of core capital in Tanzania. In contrast, with the stabilization of the financial markets, Paraguay raised the daily net operating long position to US$20 million from US$5 million. The requirement that banks sell amounts exceeding SI$10 million on trading accounts (nostro/vostro) to the Central Bank of the Solomon Islands to remain within their overnight limit was eliminated. To help mitigate liquidity challenges, banks were required to maintain a maximum of 25 percent of foreign currency account balances in nostro accounts offshore to meet day-to-day international payment obligations in Zimbabwe.

While the strengthening of the norms with respect to lending in foreign exchange continued amid concerns about the systemic risk banks' unhedged foreign currency lending to residents may pose, some countries rolled back previously introduced restrictions. For example, Austria updated prudential regulations with respect to risk management and granting of foreign-currency-denominated loans. Belarus lifted the restriction introduced in November 2012, at the height of the domestic-born crisis on foreign currency loans, except on short-term loans. Kazakhstan lifted the 20 percent provisioning requirement for foreign currency credit to borrowers without adequate foreign exchange proceeds or salary or whose foreign exchange risk was not covered by hedging instruments. In contrast, Poland introduced a 100 percent risk weight for overdue exposures secured by residential property, for which the obligation depends on changes in exchange rates or foreign currencies other than the currency of the borrower's income. Romania implemented European Systemic Risk Board Recommendations on lending in foreign currency, which require creditors to warn unhedged clients of the negative impact of exchange rate depreciation on debt obligations and to establish maximum debt-to-income ratios for consumer loans by applying a currency stress test on the debt. Conditions for lending in foreign exchange in Vietnam were significantly strengthened. Foreign exchange lending became subject to approval by the State Bank of Vietnam, and borrowers must have sufficient foreign exchange revenue to repay the foreign exchange loan.

Institutional investors

Reported changes in the regulatory framework of institutional investors do not show a clear overall direction of prudential measures and capital controls. Seventeen members reported 19 changes in prudential measures and somewhat more (21) in capital controls: a slightly higher number of changes than in the previous reporting period.

- Capital controls were mostly eased in the reporting period. The majority of the measures increased investment opportunities abroad for institutional investors (Kazakhstan, Namibia, Peru, Romania, Thailand). Limits on external transfers introduced by Cyprus in March 2013 were subsequently increased, easing the constraints on institutional investors' international operations.[29]

- Measures that tightened capital controls generally imposed stricter conditions or limits on the investment of pension funds and insurance companies abroad. These measures are considered capital controls because they discriminate against investment in foreign assets by forbidding, or setting lower limits on, institutional investors' investments abroad compared with similar investments locally. Norms on pension funds' investments were tightened in Kazakhstan, Romania, and Turkey. Foreign acquisitions of financial institutions (including banks and other financial institutions) in excess of 10 percent of total consolidated assets

---

[28] Asymmetric open foreign exchange position limits are often considered capital controls since they have the effect of influencing capital flows.

[29] Discounting the step-by-step easing of the capital outflow controls in Cyprus, the number of capital control tightening measures exceeds the number of easing measures, showing a trend similar to that of capital controls on commercial banks and other credit institutions.

became subject to approval by the minister of finance in Canada, and Bolivia reduced insurance companies' maximum investment abroad from 12 percent to 10 percent of their total investment. Restrictions were implemented in Kazakhstan on reinsurance with nonresident reinsurance organizations.

• Five reported measures (four less than in the previous reporting period) tightened the prudential framework for institutional investors' operations. The stricter conditions implemented on institutional investors' operations aim to enhance the stability of the financial system. More stringent prudential limits on institutional investors' foreign exchange position were introduced in Armenia. As part of pension reform in the Czech Republic, prudential rules for pension funds and pension companies were amended, including rules on eligible assets and investment limits and on the management of pension funds. The capital market law in Moldova redefined conditions that govern investment of funds through Undertakings for the Collective Investment of Transferable Securities (UCITS). Requirements for professional clients and qualified investors in accordance with the provisions of EU directives were also adopted. Turkey introduced new prudential rules for real estate investment companies to comply with corporate governance principles and added new obligations regarding majority shareholders.

• Four additional reported measures eased the prudential rules for investment by institutional investors. For example, pension funds and insurance companies in Bolivia were allowed to invest in Bolivian government securities issued abroad. Turkey implemented measures to support investment in private debt securities and to introduce new investment instruments and relax investment limits for mutual, hedge, and real estate funds.

More than half the reported changes in prudential measures specific to institutional investors are recorded as neutral (10). These changes cannot be linked directly to the easing or tightening of rules and reflect mainly institutional or procedural changes. New laws were adopted and existing regulations consolidated in Argentina and Kosovo. The amendment of the pension security law in Kazakhstan defined the competence of government agencies in the field of pensions and clarified the provisions for pension annuities. In Lithuania, a shift of supervisory responsibilities to the Bank of Lithuania required some changes in the regulations. In Turkey, the capital markets law was amended to comply with the UCITS regulations, increase effectiveness and competitiveness, and comply with changes and improvements in the financial sector.

Special Topic

Assessing Macroprudential Policies in a Financial Stability Framework

The global financial crisis revealed imbalances and vulnerabilities that had built up across the financial system during the preceding boom, including opaque interconnections among financial firms and the procyclical buildup of high debt and excessive leverage. These systemwide financial vulnerabilities, or systemic risks, were beyond the control of traditional "microprudential" financial regulation and supervision measures, which focus on individual institutions. They also arose during a period of relative economic and price stability.

Some time before the crisis, policymakers began to recognize the danger of systemic imbalances, particularly the buildup of credit booms, and discussed various "macroprudential," or systemwide, approaches for containing them. The crisis forcefully illustrated that systemic risks could develop across institutions as well as cyclically and refocused the attention of policymakers and international institutions on the issue. Since the crisis, regulatory reforms have created new macroprudential structures and tools to identify and mitigate such systemic risks and thereby better protect the broader economy.

Systemic Risk

Systemic risk refers to the chance that large parts of the financial system may cease functioning and thereby disrupt the real economy (IMF, 2013b). Such disruption can arise from three basic threats to financial institutions: (1) excessive common exposures to risky asset holdings that can weaken the ability of the system to provide services when risks materialize (a systemic amplification of shocks); (2) credit booms fueled by procyclical linkages of asset prices and credit (the overexposure of all institutions to shocks); and (3) linkages within the financial system, arising from cross-exposures between institutions, that render certain intermediaries "too interconnected to fail" (a vulnerability to linkages).

Under any of those conditions, a major shock to the financial sector may trigger a cascade of problems across intermediaries—as exemplified by the bursting of the house price bubble in the United States in the run-up to the global financial crisis. If the affected financial institutions react by engaging in a fire sale of assets and pulling back on lending the result is a brake on activity in the real economy (IMF/BIS/FSB, 2009). Recovery from recessions caused by such financial crises takes a relatively long time because of the legacy of high debt levels and a weakened credit system.

In the event that financial institutions become vulnerable to linkages (the third threat), the failure of a single institution could generate systemic contagion through any of several channels, including the direct exposure of other institutions to the failed institution; a loss in the value of commonly held assets; a loss of funding, payment, hedging, or other services formerly provided by the institution; and a general spike in funding costs (runs), especially if there is uncertainty about the extent of risk or the level of exposure within the financial system (Nier, 2011).

The Origins of Macroprudential Policy

Systemic risk is mitigated through the use of macroprudential tools and policies. These are distinguished from macroeconomic policy, which encompasses the economy-wide levers of fiscal and monetary policy. And they are distinguished from microprudential oversight: although both micro- and macroprudential policies seek to constrain excessive risk taking by financial intermediaries, microprudential regulation promotes the stability and soundness of individual firms in order to protect investors, most notably insured depositors, and prevent losses to the taxpayer-backed deposit insurance agency. The goal of macroprudential regulation is to maintain the stability and resilience of the overall financial system, and hence shield the broader economy, by mitigating systemic risk primarily by preventing a major disruption in the provision of financial services (IMF 2011).

The macroprudential concept emerged about 35 years ago, in the context of the first threat listed above—common exposure to risky asset holdings, specifically to developing country debt. Early uses of the term generally referred to the regulated banking system, but the scope of macroprudential policy today is much broader.

A history prepared for the Bank for International Settlements (BIS) traces the first use of the term to the unpublished minutes of a June 1979 meeting about the macroeconomic risks of the rapid increase then under way in international lending to developing economies (Clement, 2010, p. 60). According to these minutes, the meeting's chairman, W.P. Cooke, of the Bank of England, said,

> micro-economic problems … began to merge into macro-economic problems … at the point where micro-prudential problems became what could be called macro-prudential ones. The Committee had a justifiable concern with [the link between] macro-prudential problems and … macro-economic ones.[30]

The following year, the Lamfalussy Working Party report to the April 1980 meeting of the Group of 10 (G10) central bank governors urged "effective supervision of the international banking system, from both the micro-prudential and the macro-prudential points of view."[31]

The term "macroprudential" was used in a public document in 1986, apparently for the first time, but not again until 1992. In each case, it appeared in reports from the Euro-currency Standing Committee (ECSC) of the G10 central banks, each report examining the risks to the financial system posed by financial innovations, including in derivatives markets and securitization. For the 1992 report, the G10 governors asked the ECSC to focus on "the role and interaction of banks in non-traditional markets, … the linkages among various segments of the interbank markets and among the players active in them, and to consider the macro-prudential concerns to which these aspects might give rise." (Clement, 2010, p. 62)

Another relatively early public use came in a 1998 IMF report examining supervisory approaches to "institutions that have the potential to create systemic problems domestically or internationally" (IMF, 1998, pp. 3 and 13):

> Effective bank supervision … is mainly achieved through … both micro- and macro-prudential [monitoring] … Macro-prudential analysis is based on market intelligence and macroeconomic information, and focuses on developments in important asset markets, other financial intermediaries, and macroeconomic developments and potential imbalances.[32]

An influential discussion of the concept came in a 2000 speech by BIS General Manager Andrew Crockett, who said that systemic financial risk arises from the aggregate actions of financial institutions (a phenomenon beyond the scope of microprudential regulation) and that the goal of macroprudential policy is to protect the macroeconomy by limiting those risks. Moreover, he declared, systemic risk has a "time dimension," in which expansions and contractions in the financial system and the real economy are mutually reinforcing (a feature later termed procyclicality); and a "cross-sectional" (now also termed structural) dimension of risks across institutions (Crockett, 2000).

In the years between the Crockett speech and the global financial crisis, notes Clement (2010, p. 65), "the policy debate had focused largely on the time dimension" and on countercyclical capital standards. "Following the crisis, however, the cross-sectional dimension also came to the fore, mainly as a result of concerns over systemically significant institutions and the associated 'too big to fail' problem."

---

[30] The meeting was of the Committee on Banking Regulations and Supervisory Practices (the Cooke Committee), a forerunner of the Basel Committee on Banking Supervision.

[31] An October 1979 background paper for the report noted that macroprudential policy "considers problems that bear upon the market as a whole as distinct from an individual bank, and which may not be obvious at the micro-prudential level." But the term "macroprudential" was not used in the public communiqué from the April 1980 G10 meeting, in part because of "the reluctance of the Cooke Committee to use prudential measures with a macroprudential focus" (Clement, 2010, pp. 61–62).

[32] "Systemic risk" is, according to Dwyer (2009), "a relatively new term that has its origin in policy discussions, not the professional economics and finance literature." According to Dwyer's search of the EconLit database, its first appearance in the economics and finance literature (as opposed to policy literature) was in 1994, in the title of a book review.

The Scope of Macroprudential Policy

Macroprudential policy must address the systemic risks stemming from all three of the threats listed above: the potential for shocks to be amplified, the overexposure of financial institutions to shocks, and the system's vulnerability to linkages (particularly, the existence of institutions that are too big or too interconnected to fail). As a result, macroprudential policy must address both aggregate imbalances and imbalances that occur in individual, systemically important financial institutions (SIFIs), including nonbank financial institutions. Limiting aggregate imbalances implies macroprudential oversight of all leveraged providers of credit, including nonbank institutions such as finance companies and money market mutual funds because, in the aggregate, they can pose amplification and overexposure risk (Nier, 2011). And the rise of market-based corporate finance, banks' use of wholesale funding, and more globalized finance mean that SIFIs include not just large banks but firms such as payment and insurance service providers.[33] This implies that a potentially diverse range of regulatory agencies must be involved in the creation and implementation of macroprudential policy, not only in advanced economies but also increasingly in emerging market economies that are deepening their financial sectors.

The Limits of Macroprudential Policy

IMF (2013b) notes in an overview that the "use of macroprudential policy tools is growing rapidly, and many countries are striving to build appropriate institutional underpinnings for such policies, [but] the macroprudential policy framework remains work in progress." As for any type of public policy, if the purposes of macroprudential policy are not clear, the results will fall short. Current work is focused on carefully delineating the important tasks for macroprudential policy from those to be achieved through other stability frameworks.

Most broadly, macroprudential policy should not be used to achieve objectives that are not closely related to systemic vulnerabilities. It is no substitute for macroeconomic management, which is in the realm of fiscal and monetary policy (although their effects on systemic risk, both positive and negative, are being increasingly studied), nor is it a tool to allocate credit or alter market rigidities.

For example, macroprudential policy tools can mitigate the systemic vulnerabilities produced by unsustainable capital flows or excessive exchange rate exposures. But it is the task of a different set of tools, capital flow measures (CFMs), to directly affect the level or direction of flows, even though these should not substitute for warranted macroeconomic policy adjustments. Inevitably, however, the two realms overlap, and the deployment of CFMs is often seen as an exercise in macroprudential control (Blanchard, Dell'Ariccia, and Mauro, 2013).

Another example is the problem of a run-up in the prices of securities and other assets (including the exchange rate insofar as it is an asset price). "Since these prices are likely to be driven by a range of fundamental and speculative factors—including other policies—affecting them should not be seen as a primary aim of macroprudential policies," according to IMF (2013b). The question to be addressed with macroprudential policy is the extent to which sustained price increases are likely to be accompanied at some point by an increase in the vulnerability of the financial system. Such vulnerability may take the form of an unusual rise in the credit-to-GDP ratio or heavy exposure to particular sectors. In those cases, macroprudential policy may increase the resilience of the financial system to a price shock.

Nonetheless, macroprudential policy in practice overlaps with both the traditional prudential oversight framework and the systemwide scope of monetary policy. A key aspect of designing a macroprudential capability is preserving the independence of all three frameworks while ensuring that they work in concert.

---

[33] The interagency Financial Stability Oversight Council was created in the United States by the Dodd-Frank Act of 2010 in part to identify specific nonbanks that should receive oversight (by the Federal Reserve) to preserve systemic stability. In July 2013 it announced its first selections of nonbank SIFIs: the insurance provider American International Group (AIG) and the nonbank lender General Electric Capital. According to the announcement, "the Council determined that material financial distress at these companies—if it were to occur—could pose a threat to U.S. financial stability" (www.treasury.gov/press-center/press-releases/Pages/jl2004.aspx).

Macroprudential policy is a complement to microprudential policy and it interacts with other types of public policy that have an impact on systemic financial stability. Indeed, prudential regulation, as carried out in the past, also had some macroprudential aspects, and the recent crisis has reinforced this focus; hence, a clear separation between "micro" and "macro" prudential, if useful conceptually, is difficult to delineate in practice. ... This calls for coordination across policies, to ensure that systemic risk is comprehensively addressed. (IMF, 2011, p. 3)

With regard to the coordination of macro- with microprudential policies, a June 2013 IMF paper (Osiński, Seal, and Hoogduin, 2013) recommends a clear separation of "mandates, functions, and toolkits" so as to limit the potential for conflict between the systemwide and institution-specific aspects of the two frameworks, respectively. This paper cautions, however, that as the credit cycle nears what will later be seen as its expansionary peak, macroprudential policy may call for restraint at the same time that restraint seems least necessary from the micro perspective.

However, "The differences between the two policies are at their most stark in the downswing when they can have diverging assessments of the extent to which buffers may be released to contain excessive deleveraging without endangering the stability of individual institutions, as well as the extent of consequences of a potential deleveraging induced by microprudential policy actions" (Osiński, Seal, and Hoogduin, 2013, p. 15). In all cases, it is fundamental that there be discussion among the relevant authorities based on common information and "participation to the extent possible in each other's decision-making" in order to ensure a consistent and effective approach to stability management (p. 13).

Likewise, coordination with monetary policy is essential. In an ideal world, macroprudential policy would be able to eliminate excessive risk in the financial system, releasing monetary policy to focus on the stability of prices and output. However, even in this ideal scenario, macroprudential and monetary policy would affect each other (IMF, 2013a). In practice, the distinction is even less clear-cut. Monetary policy often must be used to achieve some aspects of financial stabilization. "Similarly, where monetary policy is constrained, as within currency unions and in many small open economies, there will be greater demands on macroprudential policies."

Indicators and Tools

The IMF has been monitoring and analyzing the postcrisis development of systemic risk indicators, macroprudential tools, and institutional frameworks to aid policymakers in shaping them to best fit national circumstances and international challenges.[34] No single indicator of systemic risk has been identified as decisive, and so macroprudential policy must rely on a range of indicators. The pace or extent of credit growth, for example, are insufficient on their own to indicate whether such credit growth poses a systemic risk. In an econometric study of potential macroprudential indicators and tools, Chapter 3 of the IMF's September 2011 *Global Financial Stability Report* (GFSR) finds that both credit growth and the ratio of credit to GDP provide strong to moderately strong advance signals of an impending banking crisis. It recommends, however, that authorities augment their use of those indicators by seeking to detect increases in other key indicators (a recommendation echoed in IMF, 2013b, which includes among the complementary indicators asset prices, leverage, lending standards, debt service indicators, interest rate and currency risks, and external imbalances).

Measures of capital and liquidity strength, derived in part through stress tests of institutions, can also indicate cyclical problems. And new measurement techniques (network analysis and contingent claims analysis) can help identify a buildup of structural risks related to interconnectedness, although the authorities will need improved data to take full advantage of those techniques (IMF, 2013b).

---

[34] As noted in Lim and others (2011, p. 7), the IMF Executive Board in April 2011 asked for further work on macroprudential issues in four areas: (1) identifying indicators of systemic risk (addressed in Chapter 3 of the September 2011 *Global Financial Stability Report*—GFSR); (2) reviewing country experiences on the use and effectiveness of macroprudential instruments (covered in Lim and others, 2011); (3) assessing the effectiveness of different institutional setups for macroprudential policy (done in Nier and others, 2011); and (4) assessing the multilateral aspects of macroprudential policy (covered in IMF, 2013b).

Macroprudential tools, some of which have been in use in emerging market economies since before the global financial crisis,[35] broadly encompass three sets of tools: (1) countercyclical capital buffers and provisions; (2) tools that target exposures to particular sectors, such as limits on loan-to-value and debt-to income ratios; and (3) liquidity tools, such as liquidity and reserve requirements, to contain funding risks from rapid increases in credit (IMF 2013b).

According to IMF 2013b, these three sets of tools can reinforce and complement each other in addressing the buildup of risks through time. Interlocking use of these tools can help overcome the shortcomings of any one single tool and enable policymakers to adjust the overall policy response to a range of risk profiles.

Lim and others (2011) find that several tools are effective in limiting a buildup of financial risk taking: caps on the loan-to-value and debt-to-income ratios, liquidity requirements, and dynamic (countercyclical) loan-loss provisioning. The effects of countercyclical capital buffers are less evident, possibly because there are fewer observations of them than for the other tools during the sample period (2000–10). The results on effectiveness are independent of the type of exchange rate regime in place (see also IMF, 2013b, for a comprehensive account of tools, calibration, and regulatory and data gaps).

The use of reserve requirements as a macroprudential tool in Latin America was addressed in an IMF working paper that notes their "flexibility, widespread use, and scope" (Tovar, Garcia-Escribano, and Martin, 2012). The paper finds that macroprudential use of reserve requirements over the 2003–11 period had a moderate but transitory effect on credit growth. It also finds that the use of monetary and macroprudential instruments in Latin America, including reserve requirements, appears to have been complementary in recent cases.

Capital flow measures, which include capital controls as well as micro- and macroprudential tools, are intended to stem capital inflows, which can in turn fuel credit growth and exchange appreciation. An IMF review (Habermeier, Kokenyne, and Baba, 2011) finds that "for reasons that are not yet fully understood, capital controls and related prudential measures achieve their stated objectives in some cases but not in others, and it is not possible to draw definitive conclusions. Close attention needs to be given to the choice and design of such measures." The issue of design is addressed in Ostry and others (2011).

The revised international standard for the regulation of banking, known as Basel III and issued in December 2010 by the Basel Committee on Banking Supervision (BCBS, 2010), embodies significant macroprudential elements for the oversight of banks. Basel III recommendations include phased-in requirements for higher and cyclically adjustable capital buffers, a leverage ratio, first-ever standards for liquidity and stabilized funding of assets. The Basel Committee is also addressing risk management, particularly when banks trade on their own account, for which it is proposing higher capital requirements and stricter isolation from core banking. In addition, the Basel Committee has revised its *Core Principles for Effective Banking Supervision* (BCBS, 2012) to emphasize the need for a macroprudential perspective and for better resolution mechanisms. The IMF and World Bank use the Basel Committee core principles as part of the Financial Sector Assessment Program, which evaluates countries' prudential oversight of banking.

Mitigating the problem of "too big to fail" includes proposals for capital surcharges on institutions, efforts to separate "core" banking from riskier activities, and work on devising more effective resolution mechanisms for intermediaries to minimize the need for taxpayer funds in dealing with insolvency.

Another class of tools consist of structural changes to payment, settlement, and clearing systems to prevent the buildup of hidden counterparty credit risks such as those that occurred before the global financial crisis with bilateral transactions in customized derivatives (IMF, 2013b). Centralized counterparties that settle standardized products would introduce transparency and greater market discipline. (They have an incentive to monitor the condition of their counterparties and insist on having positions marked to market.) But they also concentrate risk and so themselves must be subject to close regulatory oversight. The safety of their operations, and of course of the entire financial system, would also be enhanced by requirements for greater transparency on the part of financial institutions.

---

[35] See the Special Topic in the 2011 *Annual Report on Exchange Arrangements and Exchange Restrictions* on "Policy Responses for Managing Large Capital Inflows."

Institutional Frameworks

Implementation of the broader institutional scope of the macroprudential view requires new institutional arrangements. A key feature of any formal financial stability mechanism is "an authority with a clear mandate for macroprudential policy; and a formal mechanism of coordination or consultation across policies aimed at financial stability" (IMF, 2011, p. 12). A number of jurisdictions have passed major legislation since the crisis to create such arrangements. A central goal of the initiatives is to create an explicit macroprudential policy function that integrates macroprudential oversight and tools within existing prudential and monetary policy frameworks (IMF, 2011, p. 36; and Box 3.1 of the September 2011 GFSR).

The appropriate macroprudential framework depends on country circumstances. IMF (2013b) finds three models are being increasingly used in practice and that all three share these desirable characteristics: a designated body is responsible for macroprudential policy, and the central bank is a participant if not the leader. The models are described in the report as follows:

- Model 1: The macroprudential mandate is assigned to the central bank, with macroprudential decisions ultimately made by its board (as in the Czech Republic).

- Model 2: The macroprudential mandate is assigned to a dedicated committee within the central bank structure (as in Malaysia and the United Kingdom).

- Model 3: The macroprudential mandate is assigned to a committee outside the central bank, with the central bank participating on the macroprudential committee (as in Australia, France, Germany, and the United States).

The European Union follows model 3, with the president of the European Central Bank serving as head of the European Systemic Risk Board, which coordinates macroprudential policy across all member countries.

Latin America, historically a region highly prone to banking crises, is also making strides in establishing dedicated macroprudential policy bodies. Many countries in the region have long used macroprudential tools to address credit and exchange rate surges, and many have gradually strengthened their prudential oversight of banking. But only a few—Chile, Mexico, and Uruguay—have implemented explicit multi-institutional arrangements for maintaining systemic financial stability. (The governing board of the central bank of Brazil has created a committee of the whole that is tasked with the responsibility for macroprudential stability.)

Jácome, Nier, and Imam (2012) examine current and potential stability structures in eight Latin American countries. In five, dubbed the "Pacific" group—Chile, Colombia, Costa Rica, Peru, and Mexico—oversight of banking institutions is located outside the central bank; and in three (the "Atlantic" group)—Argentina, Brazil, and Uruguay—such oversight is lodged within the central bank.[36] The study suggests that the coordinating committees established in Chile and Mexico represent an appropriate path for other countries in the Pacific group to tie together the efforts of their disparate oversight agencies, but that any such committee needs power—those in Chile and Mexico can only make recommendations.

In the Atlantic group, where the central bank directs both monetary policy and prudential oversight, the authors find the main challenge is to assign clear macroprudential accountability to the oversight function. "It would ... seem desirable to introduce the pursuit of financial stability as the main objective of the central bank's actions in supervision and regulation" (p. 30).

International Coordination

The fact that finance is highly globalized means that macroprudential policy in each country must have a multilateral perspective and capacity. The buildup of imbalances in any single country must be addressed multilaterally lest a form of cross-border arbitrage take hold. If only a single country or a small group of countries adjust policy, lending can take place through a subsidiary institution in one country while being recorded on the books of the parent in another. Basel III already calls for international coordination in the adjustment of countercyclical capital buffers (so that, when the buffer "is activated in any given country, all

---

[36] Banks are the dominant financial institutions in Latin America. Even in the Atlantic group of countries, oversight of other financial services, including insurance and securities trading, is handled by authorities outside the central bank.

countries are meant to apply the buffer to exposures into that country"), and such reciprocity arrangements must be expanded to other tools (IMF, 2013b). International coordination is also critical for resolving home-host issues with regard to financial institutions that have affiliates in multiple jurisdictions and to achieve effective resolution of internationally active institutions.

The ability of national authorities to take action that may be controversial in their home countries can be strengthened by broadened surveillance of national frameworks by international bodies such as the IMF, as well as by guidance from the Basel Committee on Banking Supervision and the Financial Stability Board (FSB). The IMF is well placed to facilitate further work on macroprudential policy and, "through its existing programs of surveillance, [Financial Sector Assessment Program reviews], and technical assistance, to help countries conduct an in-depth assessment of systemic risks, and to advise on preventive macroprudential action in the light of this assessment" (IMF, 2013b).

The FSB is an international committee of officials from monetary and financial supervisory agencies established by the Group of 20 (G20) to "coordinate at the international level the work of national financial authorities and international standard setting bodies" and to promote effective policies for the financial sector. Notably, its charter states that part of its mandate is to assess financial sector vulnerabilities and review actions needed to address them "within a macroprudential perspective."[37] Under a mandate from the G20, the FSB and IMF jointly conduct the Early Warning Exercise program to assess low-probability, high-impact risks to the global economy and the means to address them.

Outlook

Blanchard, Dell'Ariccia, and Mauro (2013) conclude that the mutual relationship among monetary, fiscal, and macroprudential policies is still "vague" and in flux. Central banks could emerge as the center of both monetary and macroprudential policy, with the independence of the monetary authority providing political cover to the potentially more contentious application of macroprudential tools. However, if the macroprudential measures are perceived to somehow threaten the independence of the monetary authority, at the extreme, the result could be a suppression of the use of such macroprudential tools.[38] In that case, with the need for financial stability management no less urgent, the monetary authority might find itself moving toward a flexible inflation rate policy to cover the roles that arguably would be better played by macroprudential and fiscal tools.

The IMF (2013b) offers three conclusions about the relationship of macroprudential and macroeconomic policies:

- **The policy framework should not overburden macroprudential policy.** Macroprudential policy cannot cure all ills. For it to make a contribution to macroeconomic stability, its objectives must be defined clearly and in a manner that can form the basis of a strong accountability framework.

- **Macroprudential policy must be complemented by strong macroeconomic policies.** Prudential policies alone are unlikely to be effective in containing systemic risk driven by real imbalances. Macroeconomic policies are needed too, including monetary, fiscal and structural policies.

- **Macroprudential policy should not be expected to prevent all future crises.** Policymakers need to accept that crises will continue to occur and be prepared to manage these crises through appropriate policies.

The IMF also identifies some important areas for further work, including the development of better leading indicators to signal when systemic risk is building, more reliable criteria for deciding when to take action, and a better understanding of financial system behavior in the aftermath of shocks.

---

[37] See www.financialstabilityboard.org.

[38] A recent review of macroprudential policies at central banks noted that "the new instruments may prove politically treacherous in practice. Using interest rates to steer an economy, while sometimes controversial, is widely accepted by markets, banks, politicians and the public. Making it hard for families to buy homes isn't. When Israel's central bank boosted the minimum down payment on a home to 30 percent, it made it 25 percent for first-time home buyers" (Wessel and Frangos, 2013).

Finally, macroprudential policies involve trade-offs. And there can be unintended consequences of using countercyclical and sectoral policies, particularly when there are gaps in the available data. The use of such policies may raise the cost of financial intermediation and induce financial institutions to relocate or shift their organizational structure to exploit regulatory gaps. As a result, macroprudential authorities must consider such dynamic factors and the limits of the available data when they assess the potential costs and benefits of action. And once tools are deployed, the authorities must likewise monitor developments to assess the policies' effectiveness and to look for unanticipated shifts in financial system behavior and structure. These challenges are among the reasons the IMF emphasizes that "A strong institutional framework is essential to ensure that macroprudential policy can work effectively" (IMF 2013b).

References

Basel Committee on Banking Supervision (BCBS), 2010, *Basel III: A Global Regulatory Framework for More Resilient Banks and Banking Systems* (Basel). www.bis.org/publ/bcbs189_dec2010.htm.

_____, 2012, *Core Principles for Effective Banking Supervision* (Basel). www.bis.org/publ/bcbs230.htm

Blanchard, Olivier, Giovanni Dell'Ariccia, and Paolo Mauro, 2013, Rethinking Macro Policy II: Getting Granular, IMF Staff Discussion Note No. 13/03 (Washington: International Monetary Fund), www.imf.org/external/pubs/ft/sdn/2013/sdn1303.pdf.

Clement, Piet, 2010, "The Term 'Macroprudential': Origins and Evolution," *BIS Quarterly Review* (Basel). www.bis.org/publ/qtrpdf/r_qt1003h.htm.

Crockett, Andrew D., 2000, "Marrying the Micro- and Macro-Prudential Dimensions of Financial Stability," speech to the Eleventh International Conference of Banking Supervisors, Basel, September 20–21. www.bis.org/speeches/sp000921.htm.

Dwyer, Gerald P., 2009, "What Is Systemic Risk, Anyway?" Macroblog, Federal Reserve Bank of Atlanta, November 6. http://macroblog.typepad.com/macroblog/2009/11/what-is-systemic-risk-anyway.html.

Habermeier, Karl, Annamaria Kokenyne, and Chikako Baba, 2011, "The Effectiveness of Capital Controls and Prudential Policies in Managing Large Inflows," IMF Staff Discussion Note No. 11/14 (Washington: International Monetary Fund).

International Monetary Fund (IMF), 1998, Toward a Framework for Financial Stability, World Economic and Financial Surveys (Washington). www.imf.org/external/pubs/ft/wefs/toward/pdf/file01.pdf and file03.pdf.

_____, 2011, "Macroprudential Policy: An Organizing Framework," IMF Policy Paper (Washington: International Monetary Fund). www.imf.org/external/np/pp/eng/2011/031411.pdf.

_____, 2013a, "The Interaction of Monetary and Macroprudential Policies," IMF Policy Paper (Washington: International Monetary Fund). www.imf.org/external/np/pp/eng/2013/012913.pdf.

_____, 2013b, "Key Aspects of Macroprudential Policy," IMF Policy Paper No. 13/145 (Washington: International Monetary Fund).

International Monetary Fund (IMF), Bank for International Settlements (BIS), and Financial Stability Board (FSB), 2009, *Guidance to Assess the Systemic Importance of Financial Institutions, Markets and Instruments: Initial Considerations,* Report to the G20 Finance Ministers and Central Bank Governors, October 28,. www.imf.org/external/np/g20/pdf/100109.pdf.

Jácome, Luis I., Erlend W. Nier, and Patrick Imam, 2012, "Building Blocks for Effective Macroprudential Policies in Latin America: Institutional Considerations," IMF Working Paper No. 12/183 (Washington: International Monetary Fund).

Lim, C., F. Columba, A. Costa, P. Kongsamut, A. Otani, M. Saiyid, T. Wezel, and X. Wu, 2011, "Macroprudential Policy: What Instruments and How to Use Them? Lessons from Country Experiences," IMF Working Paper No. 11/238 (Washington: International Monetary Fund).

Nier, Erlend W., 2011, "Macroprudential Policy—Taxonomy and Challenges," *National Institute Economic Review,* Vol. 216, No. 1, pp. R1–R15.

————, Jacek Osiński, Luis I. Jácome, and Pamela Madrid, 2011, "Towards Effective Macroprudential Policy Frameworks: An Assessment of Stylized Institutional Models," IMF Working Paper No. 11/250 (Washington: International Monetary Fund).

Osiński, Jacek, Katharine Seal, and Lex Hoogduin, 2013, Macroprudential and Microprudential Policies: Toward Cohabitation, IMF Staff Discussion Note No. 13/05 (Washington: International Monetary Fund).

Ostry, Jonathan D., Atish R. Ghosh, Karl Habermeier, Luc Laeven, Marcos Chamon, Mahvash S. Qureshi, and Annamaria Kokenyne, 2011, "Managing Capital Inflows: What Tools to Use?" IMF Staff Position Note No. 11/06 (Washington: International Monetary Fund).

Tovar, Camilo E., Mercedes Garcia-Escribano, and Mercedes Vera Martin, 2012. "Credit Growth and the Effectiveness of Reserve Requirements and Other Macroprudential Instruments in Latin America," IMF Working Paper No. 12/142 (Washington: International Monetary Fund).

Wessel, David, and Alex Frangos, 2013, "Central Bankers Hone Tools to Pop Bubbles." http://online.wsj.com. July 8.

Compilation Guide

Status under IMF Articles of Agreement

Article VIII
The member country has accepted the obligations of Article VIII, Sections 2, 3, and 4, of the IMF's Articles of Agreement.

Article XIV
The member country continues to avail itself of the transitional arrangements of Article XIV, Section 2.

Exchange Measures

Restrictions and/or multiple currency practices
Exchange restrictions and multiple currency practices (MCPs) maintained by a member country under Article VIII, Sections 2, 3, and 4, or under Article XIV, Section 2, of the IMF's Articles of Agreement, as specified in the latest IMF staff reports issued as of December 31, 2012. Information on exchange restrictions and MCPs or on the absence of exchange restrictions and MCPs for countries with unpublished staff reports is published only with the consent of the authorities. If no consent has been received, the *Annual Report on Exchange Agreements and Exchange Restrictions* (AREAER) indicates "Information is not publicly available." Hence, "Information is not publicly available" does not necessarily imply that the country maintains exchange restrictions or MCPs. It indicates only that the country's relevant staff report has not been published and the authorities have not consented to publication of information on the existence of exchange restrictions and MCPs. Because in some cases the relevant staff document refers to years before the reporting period of the AREAER, more recent changes in the exchange system may not be included in those staff reports. Changes in the category restrictions and/or multiple currency practices are reflected in the subsequent edition of the AREAER, which covers the calendar year during which the IMF staff report with information on such changes is issued. Changes in the measures giving rise to exchange restrictions or MCPs that affect other categories of the country tables are reported under the relevant categories in the AREAER in accordance with the standard reporting periods.

Exchange measures imposed for security reasons
Exchange measures on payments and transfers in connection with international transactions imposed by member countries for reasons of national or international security.

In accordance with IMF Executive Board Decision No. 144-(52/51)
Security restrictions on current international payments and transfers on the basis of IMF Executive Board Decision No. 144-(52/51), which establishes the obligation of members to notify the IMF before imposing such restrictions, or, if circumstances preclude advance notification, as promptly as possible.

Other security restrictions
Other restrictions imposed for security reasons (e.g., in accordance with UN or EU regulations) but not notified to the IMF under Board Decision 144-(52/51).

References to legal instruments and hyperlinks
Specific references to the underlying legal materials and hyperlinks to the legal texts. The category is included at the end of each section.

Exchange Arrangement

Currency
The official legal tender of the country.

Other legal tender	The existence of another currency that is officially allowed to be used in the country.
Exchange rate structure	If there is one exchange rate, the system is called unitary; if there is more than one exchange rate that may be used simultaneously for different purposes and/or by different entities, and these exchange rates give rise to MCPs or differing rates for current and capital transactions, the system is called dual or multiple. Different effective exchange rates resulting from exchange taxes or subsidies, excessive exchange rate spreads between buying and selling rates, bilateral payments agreements, and broken cross rates are not included in this category. Changes in the measures in this category are reported in accordance with the standard reporting periods. Reclassification in cases related to changes in MCPs occurs in the edition of the AREAER that covers the calendar year during which the IMF staff report including information on such changes is issued.
Classification	Describes and classifies the de jure and the de facto exchange rate arrangements.

De jure

The description and effective dates of the de jure exchange rate arrangements are provided by the authorities. Under Article IV, Section 2(a), of the IMF's Articles of Agreement and Paragraph 16 of 2007 Surveillance Decision No. 13919-(07/51), each member is required to notify the IMF of the exchange arrangements it intends to apply and to notify the IMF promptly of any changes in its exchange arrangements. Country authorities are also requested to identify, whenever possible, which of the existing exchange rate arrangement categories listed below most closely corresponds to the de jure arrangement in effect. Country authorities may also wish to briefly describe their official exchange rate policy. The description includes officially announced or estimated parameters of the exchange arrangement (e.g., parity, bands, weights, rate of crawl, and other indicators used to manage the exchange rate). It also provides information on the computation of the exchange rate.

De facto

The IMF staff classifies the de facto exchange rate arrangements according to the categories below. The name and the definition of the categories describing the de facto exchange rate arrangements have been modified in accordance with the revised classification methodology, as of February 1, 2009. Wherever the description of the de jure arrangement can be empirically confirmed by the staff over at least the previous six months, the exchange rate arrangement is classified in the same way on a de facto basis. Because the de facto methodology for classification of exchange rate regimes is based on a backward-looking approach that relies on past exchange rate movement and historical data, some countries have been reclassified retroactively to the date the behavior of the exchange rate changed and matched the criteria for reclassification to the appropriate category. For these countries, if the retroactive date of reclassification precedes the period covered in this report, the effective date of change to be entered in the country chapter and the changes section is deemed to be the first day of the year in which the decision of reclassification took place.

No separate legal tender

Classification as an *exchange rate arrangement with no separate legal tender* involves confirmation of the country authorities' de jure exchange rate arrangement. The currency of another country circulates as the sole legal tender (formal dollarization). Adopting such an arrangement implies complete surrender of the monetary authorities' control over domestic monetary policy. Note: effective January 1, 2007, exchange arrangements of countries that belong to a monetary or currency union in which the same legal tender is shared by the members of the union are classified under the arrangement governing the joint currency. This classification is based on the behavior of the common currency, whereas the previous classification was based on the lack of a separate legal tender. The classification thus reflects only a definitional change and is not based on a judgment that there has been a substantive change in the exchange arrangement or other policies of the currency union or its members.

Currency board

Classification as a *currency board* involves confirmation of the country authorities' de jure exchange rate arrangement. A currency board arrangement is a monetary arrangement based on an explicit legislative commitment to exchange domestic currency for a specified foreign currency at a fixed exchange rate, combined with restrictions on the issuance authority to ensure the fulfillment of its legal obligation. This implies that domestic currency is usually fully backed by foreign assets, eliminating traditional central bank functions such as monetary control and lender of last resort, and leaving little room for discretionary monetary policy. Some flexibility may still be afforded, depending on the strictness of the banking rules of the currency board arrangement.

Conventional peg

Classification as a *conventional peg* involves confirmation of the country authorities' de jure exchange rate arrangement. For this category the country formally (de jure) pegs its currency at a fixed rate to another currency or a basket of currencies, where the basket is formed, for example, from the currencies of major trading or financial partners and weights reflect the geographic distribution of trade, services, or capital flows. The anchor currency or basket weights are public or notified to the IMF. The country authorities stand ready to maintain the fixed parity through direct intervention (i.e., via sale or purchase of foreign exchange in the market) or indirect intervention (e.g., via exchange-rate-related use of interest rate policy, imposition of foreign exchange regulations, exercise of moral suasion that constrains foreign exchange activity, or intervention by other public institutions). There is no commitment to irrevocably keep the parity, but the formal arrangement must be confirmed empirically: the exchange rate may fluctuate within narrow margins of less than ±1% around a central rate—or the maximum and minimum values of the spot market exchange rate must remain within a narrow margin of 2% for at least six months.

Stabilized arrangement

Classification as a *stabilized arrangement* entails a spot market exchange rate that remains within a margin of 2% for six months or more (with the exception of a specified number of outliers or step adjustments) and is not floating. The required margin of stability can be met either with respect to a single currency or a basket of currencies, where the anchor currency or the basket is ascertained or confirmed using statistical techniques. Classification as a stabilized arrangement requires that the statistical criteria are met and that the exchange rate remains stable as a result of official action (including structural market rigidities). The classification does not imply a policy commitment on the part of the country authorities.

Crawling peg	Classification as a *crawling peg* involves confirmation of the country authorities' de jure exchange rate arrangement. The currency is adjusted in small amounts at a fixed rate or in response to changes in selected quantitative indicators, such as past inflation differentials vis-à-vis major trading partners or differentials between the inflation target and expected inflation in major trading partners. The rate of crawl can be set to generate inflation-adjusted changes in the exchange rate (backward looking) or set at a predetermined fixed rate and/or below the projected inflation differentials (forward looking). The rules and parameters of the arrangement are public or notified to the IMF.
Crawl-like arrangement	For classification as a *crawl-like arrangement*, the exchange rate must remain within a narrow margin of 2% relative to a statistically identified trend for six months or more (with the exception of a specified number of outliers), and the exchange rate arrangement cannot be considered as floating. Usually, a minimum rate of change greater than allowed under a stabilized (peg-like) arrangement is required; however, an arrangement is considered crawl-like with an annualized rate of change of at least 1%, provided the exchange rate appreciates or depreciates in a sufficiently monotonic and continuous manner.
Pegged exchange rate within horizontal bands	Classification as a *pegged exchange rate within horizontal bands* involves confirmation of the country authorities' de jure exchange rate arrangement. The value of the currency is maintained within certain margins of fluctuation of at least ±1% around a fixed central rate, or a margin between the maximum and minimum value of the exchange rate that exceeds 2%. It includes arrangements of countries in the ERM of the European Monetary System, which was replaced with the ERM II on January 1, 1999, for countries with margins of fluctuation wider than ±1%. The central rate and width of the band are public or notified to the IMF.
Other managed arrangement	This category is a residual and is used when the exchange rate arrangement does not meet the criteria for any of the other categories. Arrangements characterized by frequent shifts in policies may fall into this category.
Floating	A floating exchange rate is largely market determined, without an ascertainable or predictable path for the rate. In particular, an exchange rate that satisfies the statistical criteria for a stabilized or a crawl-like arrangement is classified as such unless it is clear that the stability of the exchange rate is not the result of official actions. Foreign exchange market intervention may be either direct or indirect and serves to moderate the rate of change and prevent undue fluctuations in the exchange rate, but policies targeting a specific level of the exchange rate are incompatible with floating. Indicators for managing the rate are broadly judgmental (e.g., balance of payments position, international reserves, parallel market developments). Floating arrangements may exhibit more or less exchange rate volatility, depending on the size of the shocks affecting the economy.

Free floating	A floating exchange rate can be classified as *free floating* if intervention occurs only exceptionally and aims to address disorderly market conditions and if the authorities have provided information or data confirming that intervention has been limited to at most three instances in the previous six months, each lasting no more than three business days. If the information or data required are not available to the IMF staff, the arrangement is classified as floating. Detailed data on intervention or official foreign exchange transactions will not be requested routinely of member countries—only when other information available to the staff is not sufficient to resolve uncertainties about the appropriate classification.
Official exchange rate	Provides information on the computation of the exchange rate and the use of the official exchange rate (accounting, customs valuation purposes, foreign exchange transactions with the government).
Monetary policy framework	The category includes a brief description of the monetary policy framework in effect according to the following subcategories:
Exchange rate anchor	The monetary authority buys or sell foreign exchange to maintain the exchange rate at its predetermined level or within a range. The exchange rate thus serves as the nominal anchor or intermediate target of monetary policy. These frameworks are associated with exchange rate arrangements with no separate legal tender, currency board arrangements, pegs (or stabilized arrangements) with or without bands, crawling pegs (or crawl-like arrangements), and other managed arrangements.
Monetary aggregate target	The monetary authority uses its instruments to achieve a target growth rate for a monetary aggregate, such as reserve money, M1, or M2, and the targeted aggregate becomes the nominal anchor or intermediate target of monetary policy.
Inflation-targeting framework	This involves the public announcement of numerical targets for inflation, with an institutional commitment by the monetary authority to achieve these targets, typically over a medium-term horizon. Additional key features normally include increased communication with the public and the markets about the plans and objectives of monetary policymakers and increased accountability of the central bank for achieving its inflation objectives. Monetary policy decisions are often guided by the deviation of forecasts of future inflation from the announced inflation target, with the inflation forecast acting (implicitly or explicitly) as the intermediate target of monetary policy.
Other monetary framework	The country has no explicitly stated nominal anchor, but rather monitors various indicators in conducting monetary policy. This category is also used when no relevant information on the country is available.
Exchange tax	Foreign exchange transactions are subject to a special tax. Bank commissions charged on foreign exchange transactions are not included in this category; rather, they are listed under the exchange arrangement classification.
Exchange subsidy	Foreign exchange transactions are subsidized by using separate, nonmarket exchange rates.
Foreign exchange market	The existence of a foreign exchange market.

Spot exchange market	Institutional setting of the foreign exchange market for spot transactions and market participants. Existence and significance of the parallel market.
Operated by the central bank	The role of the central bank in providing access to foreign exchange to market participants: foreign exchange standing facility, allocation of foreign exchange to authorized dealers or other legal and private persons, management of buy or sell auctions or fixing sessions. Price determination and frequency of central bank operations.
	A foreign exchange standing facility allows market participants to buy foreign exchange from or sell it to the central bank at predetermined exchange rates at their own initiative and is usually instrumental in maintaining a hard or soft peg arrangement. The credibility of the facility depends to a large extent on the availability of foreign exchange reserves to back the facility.
	Allocation involves redistribution of foreign exchange inflows by the central bank to market participants for specific international transactions or in specific amounts (rationing). Foreign exchange allocation is often used to provide foreign exchange for strategic imports such as oil or food when foreign exchange reserves are scarce. In an allocation system, companies and individuals often transact directly with the central bank, and commercial banks may buy foreign exchange only for their clients' underlying international transactions. Purchases of foreign exchange for banks' own books typically are not permitted.
	Auctions are organized by the central bank, usually for market participants to buy and/or sell foreign exchange. Auctions can take the form of multiple-price auctions (all successful bidders pay the price they offer) or single-price auctions (all successful bidders pay the same price, which is the market-clearing/cut-off price). The authorities may exercise discretion in accepting or rejecting offers, and sometimes a floor price is determined in advance, below which offers are not accepted. The frequency of auctions depends mainly on the amount or availability of foreign exchange to be auctioned and on the role the auction plays in the foreign exchange market.
	Fixing sessions are often organized by the central bank at the early stage of market development to establish a market-clearing exchange rate. The central bank monitors the market closely and often actively participates in price formation by selling or buying during the session to achieve a certain exchange rate target. The price determined at the fixing session is often used for foreign exchange transactions outside the session and/or for accounting and valuation purposes.
Interbank market	The organization and operation of the interbank market; interventions. The existence of brokerage, over-the-counter, and market-making arrangements.
Forward exchange market	The existence of a forward exchange market; institutional arrangement and market participants.
Official cover of forward operations	Official coverage of forward operations refers to the case in which an official entity (the central bank or the government) assumes the exchange risk of certain foreign exchange transactions.

Arrangements for Payments and Receipts

Prescription of currency requirements

The official requirements affecting the selection of currency and the method of settlement for transactions with other countries. When a country has payments agreements with other countries, the terms of these agreements often lead to a prescription of currency for specified categories of payments to, and receipts from, the countries concerned. This category includes information on the use of domestic currency in transactions between residents and nonresidents, both domestically and abroad; it also indicates any restrictions on the use of foreign currency among residents.

Payments arrangements

Bilateral payments arrangements

Two countries have an agreement to prescribe specific rules for payments to each other, including cases in which private parties are also obligated to use specific currencies. These agreements can be either operative or inoperative.

Regional arrangements

More than two parties participate in a payments agreement.

Clearing agreements

The official bodies of two or more countries agree to offset with some regularity the balances that arise from payments to each other as a result of the exchange of goods, services, or—less often—capital.

Barter agreements and open accounts

The official bodies of two or more countries agree to offset exports of goods and services to one country with imports of goods and services from the same country, without payment.

Administration of control

The authorities' division of responsibility for monitoring policy, administering exchange controls, and determining the extent of delegation of powers to outside agencies (banks are often authorized to effect foreign exchange transactions).

Payments arrears

Official or private residents of a member country default on their payments or transfers in foreign exchange to nonresidents. This category includes only the situation in which domestic currency is available for residents to settle their debts, but they are unable to obtain foreign exchange—for example, because of the presence of an officially announced or unofficial queuing system; it does not cover nonpayment by private parties owing to bankruptcy of the party concerned.

Controls on trade in gold (coins and/or bullion)

Separate rules for trading in gold domestically and with foreign countries.

Controls on exports and imports of banknotes

Regulations governing the physical movement of means of payment between countries. Where information is available, the category distinguishes between separate limits for the (1) export and import of banknotes by travelers and (2) export and import of banknotes by banks and other authorized financial institutions.

Resident Accounts

Indicates whether resident accounts that are maintained in the national currency or in foreign currency, locally or abroad, are allowed and describes how they are treated and the facilities and limitations attached to such accounts. When there is more than one type of resident account, the nature and operation of the various types of accounts are also described—for example, whether residents are allowed to open foreign exchange accounts with or without approval from the exchange control authority, whether these accounts may be held domestically or abroad, and whether the balances on accounts held by residents in domestic currency may be converted into foreign currency.

Nonresident Accounts

Indicates whether local nonresident accounts maintained in the national currency or in foreign currency are allowed and describes how they are treated and the facilities and limitations attached to such accounts. When there is more than one type of nonresident account, the nature and operation of the various types of accounts are also described.

Blocked accounts
: Accounts of nonresidents, usually in domestic currency. Regulations prohibit or limit the conversion and/or transfer of the balances of such accounts.

Imports and Import Payments

Describes the nature and extent of exchange and trade restrictions on imports.

Foreign exchange budget
: Information on the existence of a foreign exchange plan, i.e., prior allocation of a certain amount of foreign exchange, usually on an annual basis, for the importation of specific types of goods and/or services; in some cases, also differentiating among individual importers.

Financing requirements for imports
: Information on specific import-financing regulations limiting the rights of residents to enter into private contracts in which the financing options differ from those in the official regulations.

Documentation requirements for release of foreign exchange for imports

Domiciliation requirements
: The obligation to domicile the transactions with a specified (usually domestic) financial institution.

Preshipment inspection
: Most often a compulsory government measure aimed at establishing the veracity of the import contract in terms of volume, quality, and price.

Letters of credit
: Parties are obligated to use letters of credit as a form of payment for their imports.

Import licenses used as exchange licenses
: Import licenses are used not for trade purposes but to restrict the availability of foreign exchange for legitimate trade.

Import licenses and other nontariff measures

Positive list
: A list of goods that may be imported.

Negative list
: A list of goods that may not be imported.

Open general licenses	Indicates arrangements whereby certain imports or other international transactions are exempt from the restrictive application of licensing requirements.
Licenses with quotas	Refers to situations in which a license for the importation of a certain good is granted but a specific limit is imposed on the amount to be imported.
Other nontariff measures	May include prohibitions on imports of certain goods from all countries or of all goods from a certain country. Several other nontariff measures are used by countries (e.g., phytosanitary examinations, setting of standards), but these are not covered fully in the report.
Import taxes and/or tariffs	A brief description of the import tax and tariff system, including taxes levied on the foreign exchange made available for imports.
Taxes collected through the exchange system	Indicates if any taxes apply to the exchange side of an import transaction.
State import monopoly	Private parties are not allowed to engage in the importation of certain products, or they are limited in their activity.

Exports and Export Proceeds

Describes restrictions on the use of export proceeds, as well as regulations on exports.

Repatriation requirements	The obligation of exporters to repatriate export proceeds.
Surrender requirements	
Surrender to the central bank	Regulations requiring the recipient of repatriated export proceeds to sell, sometimes at a specified exchange rate, any foreign exchange proceeds in return for local currency to the central bank.
Surrender to authorized dealers	Regulations requiring the recipient of repatriated export proceeds to sell, sometimes at a specified exchange rate, any foreign exchange proceeds in return for local currency to commercial banks or exchange dealers authorized for this purpose or on a foreign exchange market.
Financing requirements	Information on specific export-financing regulations limiting the rights of residents to enter into private contracts in which the financing options differ from those in the official regulations.
Documentation requirements	The same categories as in the case of imports are used.
Export licenses	Restrictions on the right of residents to export goods. These restrictions may take the form of quotas (where a certain quantity of shipment abroad is allowed) or the absence of quotas (where the licenses are issued at the discretion of the foreign trade control authority).
Export taxes	A brief description of the export tax system, including any taxes that are levied on foreign exchange earned by exporters.

Payments for Invisible Transactions and Current Transfers

Describes the procedures for effecting payments abroad in connection with current transactions in invisibles, with reference to prior approval requirements, the existence of quantitative and indicative limits, and/ or bona fide tests. Detailed information on the most common categories of transactions is provided only when regulations differ for the various categories. Indicative limits establish maximum amounts up to which the purchase of foreign exchange is allowed on declaration of the nature of the transaction, mainly for statistical purposes. Amounts above those limits are granted if the bona fide nature of the transaction is established by the presentation of appropriate documentation. Bona fide tests also may be applied to transactions for which quantitative limits have not been established.

Trade-related payments	Includes freight and insurance (including possible regulations on non-trade-related insurance payments and transfers), unloading and storage costs, administrative expenses, commissions, and customs duties and fees.
Investment-related payments	Includes profits and dividends, interest payments (including interest on debentures, mortgages, etc.), amortization of loans or depreciation of foreign direct investments, and payments and transfers of rent.
Payments for travel	Includes international travel for business, tourism, etc.
Personal payments	Includes medical expenditures abroad, study expenses abroad, pensions (including regulations on payments and transfers of pensions by both government and private pension providers on behalf of nonresidents, as well as the transfer of pensions due to residents living abroad), and family maintenance and alimony (including regulations on payments and transfers abroad of family maintenance and alimony by residents).
Foreign workers' wages	Transfer abroad of earnings by nonresidents working in the country.
Credit card use abroad	Use of credit and debit cards to pay for invisible transactions.
Other payments	Includes subscription and membership fees, authors' royalties, consulting and legal fees, etc.

Proceeds from Invisible Transactions and Current Transfers

Describes regulations governing exchange receipts derived from transactions in invisibles—including descriptions of any limitations on their conversion into domestic currency—and the use of those receipts.

Repatriation requirements	The definitions of repatriation and surrender requirements are similar to those applied to export proceeds.
Surrender requirements	
Surrender to the central bank	
Surrender to authorized dealers	
Restrictions on use of funds	Refers mainly to the limitations imposed on the use of receipts previously deposited in certain types of bank accounts.

Capital Transactions

Describes regulations influencing both inward and outward capital flows. The concept of controls on capital transactions is interpreted broadly. Thus, controls on capital transactions include prohibitions; need for prior approval, authorization, and notification; dual and multiple exchange rates; discriminatory taxes; and reserve requirements or interest penalties imposed by the authorities that regulate the conclusion or execution of transactions or transfers and the holding of assets at home by nonresidents and abroad by residents. The coverage of the regulations applies to receipts as well as to payments and to actions initiated by nonresidents and residents. In addition, because of the close association with capital transactions, information is also provided on local financial operations conducted in foreign currency, describing specific regulations in effect that limit residents' and nonresidents' issuance of securities denominated in foreign currency or, generally, limitations on contract agreements expressed in foreign exchange.

Repatriation requirements	The definitions of repatriation and surrender requirements are similar to those applied to export proceeds.
Surrender requirements	
Surrender to the central bank	
Surrender to authorized dealers	
Controls on capital and money market instruments	Refers to public offerings or private placements on primary markets or their listing on secondary markets.
On capital market securities	Refers to shares and other securities of a participating nature and bonds and other securities with an original maturity of more than one year.
Shares or other securities of a participating nature	Includes transactions involving shares and other securities of a participating nature if they are not effected for the purpose of acquiring a lasting economic interest in the management of the enterprise concerned. Investment for the purpose of acquiring a lasting economic interest is addressed under foreign direct investment.
Bonds or other debt securities	Refers to bonds and other securities with an original maturity of more than one year. The term "other debt securities" includes notes and debentures.
On money market instruments	Refers to securities with an original maturity of one year or less and includes short-term instruments, such as certificates of deposit and bills of exchange. The category also includes treasury bills and other short-term government paper, bankers' acceptances, commercial paper, interbank deposits, and repurchase agreements.
On collective investment securities	Includes share certificates and registry entries or other evidence of investor interest in an institution for collective investment, such as mutual funds, and unit and investment trusts.

Controls on derivatives and other instruments	Refers to operations in other negotiable instruments and nonsecured claims not covered under the above subsections. These may include operations in rights; warrants; financial options and futures; secondary market operations in other financial claims (including sovereign loans, mortgage loans, commercial credits, negotiable instruments originating as loans, receivables, and discounted bills of trade); forward operations (including those in foreign exchange); swaps of bonds and other debt securities; credits and loans; and other swaps (e.g., interest rate, debt/equity, equity/debt, foreign currency, and swaps of any of the instruments listed above). Controls on operations in foreign exchange without any other underlying transaction (spot or forward trading on the foreign exchange markets, forward cover operations, etc.) are also included.
Controls on credit operations	
Commercial credits	Covers operations directly linked with international trade transactions or with the rendering of international services.
Financial credits	Includes credits other than commercial credits granted by all residents, including banks, to nonresidents, or vice versa.
Guarantees, sureties, and financial backup facilities	Includes guarantees, sureties, and financial backup facilities provided by residents to nonresidents and vice versa. It also includes securities pledged for payment or performance of a contract—such as warrants, performance bonds, and standby letters of credit—and financial backup facilities that are credit facilities used as a guarantee for independent financial operations.
Controls on direct investment	Refers to investments for the purpose of establishing lasting economic relations both abroad by residents and domestically by nonresidents. These investments are essentially for the purpose of producing goods and services, and, in particular, in order to allow investor participation in the management of an enterprise. The category includes the creation or extension of a wholly owned enterprise, subsidiary, or branch and the acquisition of full or partial ownership of a new or existing enterprise that results in effective influence over the operations of the enterprise.
Controls on liquidation of direct investment	Refers to the transfer of principal, including the initial capital and capital gains, of a foreign direct investment as defined above.
Controls on real estate transactions	Refers to the acquisition of real estate not associated with direct investment, including, for example, investments of a purely financial nature in real estate or the acquisition of real estate for personal use.
Controls on personal capital transactions	Covers transfers initiated on behalf of private persons and intended to benefit other private persons. It includes transactions involving property to which the promise of a return to the owner with payments of interest is attached (e.g., loans or settlements of debt in their country of origin by immigrants) and transfers effected free of charge to the beneficiary (e.g., gifts and endowments, loans, inheritances and legacies, and emigrants' assets).

Provisions Specific to the Financial Sector

Provisions specific to commercial banks and other credit institutions	Describes regulations that are specific to these institutions, such as monetary, prudential, and foreign exchange controls. Inclusion of an entry in this category does not necessarily signify that the aim of the measure is to control the flow of capital. Some of these items (e.g., borrowing abroad, lending to nonresidents, purchase of locally issued securities denominated in foreign exchange, investment regulations) may be repetitions of entries under respective categories of controls on capital and money market instruments, on credit operations, or on direct investments, when the same regulations apply to commercial banks as well as to other residents.
Open foreign exchange position limits	Describes regulations on certain commercial bank balance sheet items (including capital) and on limits covering commercial banks' positions in foreign currencies (including gold).
Provisions specific to institutional investors	Describes controls specific to institutions, such as insurance companies, pension funds, investment firms (including brokers, dealers, or advisory firms), and other securities firms (including collective investment funds). Incorporates measures that impose limitations on the composition of the institutional investors' foreign or foreign currency assets (reserves, accounts) and liabilities (e.g., investments in equity capital of institutional investors or borrowing from nonresidents) and/or that differentiate between residents and nonresidents. Examples of such controls are restrictions on investments because of rules regarding the technical, mathematical, security, or mandatory reserves; solvency margins; premium reserve stocks; or guarantee funds of nonbank financial institutions. Inclusion of an entry in this category does not necessarily signify that the aim of the measure is to control the flow of capital.
Insurance companies	
Pension funds	
Investment firms and collective investment funds	

Listing conventions used in the report are as follows:

- When it is unclear whether a particular category or measure exists—because pertinent information is not available at the time of publication—the category is displayed with the notation "n.a."

- If a measure is known to exist but specific information on it is not available, the category is displayed with the notation "yes."

- If no measures exist on any item within a category, the category is displayed with the notation "no."

- If members have provided the IMF staff with information indicating that a category or an item is not regulated, these are marked "n.r."

- When relevant documents have not been published and the authorities have not consented to the publication of the information as included in the IMF staff report, the text reads, "Information is not publicly available."

Summary Features of Exchange Arrangements and Regulatory Frameworks for Current and Capital Transactions in IMF Member Countries
(As of date shown on first page of country chapter; symbol key at end of table)

	Total number of member countries with these features	Afghanistan	Albania	Algeria	Angola	Antigua and Barbuda	Argentina	Armenia	Australia	Austria	Azerbaijan	The Bahamas	Bahrain	Bangladesh	Barbados	Belarus	Belgium	Belize	Benin	Bhutan	Bolivia
Status under IMF Articles of Agreement Article VIII	168			•		•	•	•	•	•	•	•	•	•	•	•	•	•	•		•
Article XIV	20	•	•		•															•	
Exchange Rate Arrangements																					
No separate legal tender	13																				
Currency board	11					◊															
Conventional peg	43											◊	◊		◊			◊	▲	✚	
Stabilized arrangement	19				◊						◊										◊
Crawling peg	2																				
Crawl-like arrangement	15						◊														
Pegged exchange rate within horizontal bands	1																				
Other managed arrangement	19			∗										•		•					
Floating	35	•	•					•													
Free floating	30								•	⊕							⊕				
Exchange rate structure Dual exchange rates	17						•						•								
Multiple exchange rates	7				•																
Arrangements for Payments and Receipts Bilateral payments arrangements	68	•		•	•		•	•					•	•	•			•	•	•	
Payments arrears	29		•		•	•															
Controls on payments for invisible transactions and current transfers	97			•	•	•	•						•	•	•			•	•	•	•
Proceeds from exports and/or invisible transactions Repatriation requirements	85		•	•	•	—	•						•	•	•	•		•	•	•	
Surrender requirements	58			•	•		•						•	•	•			•	•	•	
Capital Transactions Controls on: *Capital market securities*	148		•	•	•		•	•	•		•	•	•	•	•	•	•	•	•	•	•
Money market instruments	125	•	•	•	•		•			•			•	•	•	•	•	•	•	•	•
Collective investment securities	125		•	•	•		•	•	•		•		•	•	•	•	•	•	•	•	•
Derivatives and other instruments	98		•	•	■		•	•					•	•	•	•		•	•	•	
Commercial credits	84			•									•	•				•	•	•	
Financial credits	114			•	•	•	•			•			•	•				•	•		•
Guarantees, sureties, and financial backup facilities	77			•	•		•						•	•	•			•	•	•	
Direct investment	151			•	•		•	•	•		•		•	•	•	•		•	•	•	
Liquidation of direct investment	46			•	•		•							•	•			•		•	
Real estate transactions	145	•	•	•	•	•	•	•	•		•		•	•	•	•		•	•	•	
Personal capital transactions	98		•	•	—		•			•			•	•	•			•	•	•	
Provisions specific to: *Commercial banks and other credit institutions*	168	•	•	•	◊		•	•			◊		•	•	•			•	•	•	•
Institutional investors	142		•	•	■	—	•	•	•	•	•		•	•	•	•	•	•	•	•	•

76   International Monetary Fund | October 2013

Summary Features of Exchange Arrangements and Regulatory Frameworks for Current and Capital Transactions in IMF Member Countries
(As of date shown on first country page; symbol key at end of table)

	Bosnia and Herzegovina	Botswana	Brazil	Brunei Darussalam	Bulgaria	Burkina Faso	Burundi	Cambodia	Cameroon	Canada	Cape Verde	Central African Republic	Chad	Chile	China	Colombia	Comoros	Dem. Rep. of the Congo	Republic of Congo	Costa Rica	Côte d'Ivoire	Croatia
Status under IMF Articles of Agreement Article VIII		•	•	•	•	•		•	•	•	•	•	•	•	•	•	•	•	•	•	•	•
Article XIV	•						•															
Exchange Rate Arrangements																						
No separate legal tender																						
Currency board	▲			+	▲																	
Conventional peg						▲			▲		▲	▲	▲				▲		▲		▲	
Stabilized arrangement								◊										◊		◊		
Crawling peg		*																				
Crawl-like arrangement															◊							▲
Pegged exchange rate within horizontal bands																						
Other managed arrangement							•														•	
Floating			•													•						
Free floating										•				•								
Exchange rate structure Dual exchange rates							•															
Multiple exchange rates																						
Arrangements for Payments and Receipts Bilateral payments arrangements		•	•		•	•	•	•			•						•					•
Payments arrears						−		•			•							•	•		•	
Controls on payments for invisible transactions and current transfers	•			•		•	•		•		•	•	•		•	•	•	•		•		
Proceeds from exports and/or invisible transactions Repatriation requirements	•					•	•	•	•			•	•		•	•	•	•	•	•		
Surrender requirements		•				•		•	•			•	•	•			•		•	•		
Capital Transactions Controls on: *Capital market securities*	•	•	•		•	•	−	•	•			•	•	•	•	•	•	•	•		•	•
Money market instruments	•	•	•			•	−	•				•	•	•	•	•		•	•		•	•
Collective investment securities	•	•	•			•	−	•				•	•	•	•	•		•	•		•	•
Derivatives and other instruments		•				•	•		■			■	■	•	•	•	•	•	■		•	•
Commercial credits		•				•	•		•			•	•			•	•		•		•	
Financial credits	•	•				•	•		•			•	•	•	•	•	•	•	•	•	•	
Guarantees, sureties, and financial backup facilities						•	•					•	■	■	•	•	•	•	•	■	•	
Direct investment	•		•		•	•	•	•	•			•	•	•	•	•	•	•	•	•	•	
Liquidation of direct investment									•			•	•		•	•		•	•	•		
Real estate transactions	•		•	•	•	•	•	•	•			•	•	•	•	•		•	•		•	•
Personal capital transactions	•					•	•	•	•			•	•		•	•		•	•	•		
Provisions specific to: *Commercial banks and other credit institutions*	•	•	•	•	•	•	•	•	•	•	•	•	•	•	•	•	•	•	•	•	•	•
Institutional investors	•	•	•	•	•	•			•	•	−	•	•	•	•	•	−		•	•	•	•

Summary Features of Exchange Arrangements and Regulatory Frameworks for Current and Capital Transactions in IMF Member Countries
(As of date shown on first page of country chapter; symbol key at end of table)

	Cyprus	Czech Republic	Denmark	Djibouti	Dominica	Dominican Republic	Ecuador	Egypt	El Salvador	Equatorial Guinea	Eritrea	Estonia	Ethiopia	Fiji	Finland	France	Gabon	The Gambia	Georgia	Germany	Ghana	Greece
Status under IMF Articles of Agreement Article VIII	•	•	•	•	•	•	•	•	•	•		•		•	•	•	•	•	•	•	•	•
Article XIV											•		•									
Exchange Rate Arrangements																						
No separate legal tender							◊		◊													
Currency board				◊	◊																	
Conventional peg			❖							▲	◊			*				▲				
Stabilized arrangement																			◊			
Crawling peg																						
Crawl-like arrangement						◊		◊					◊									
Pegged exchange rate within horizontal bands																						
Other managed arrangement																						
Floating																		•			•	
Free floating	⊕	•										⊕			⊕	⊕				⊕		⊕
Exchange rate structure Dual exchange rates											•								•		•	
Multiple exchange rates																						
Arrangements for Payments and Receipts Bilateral payments arrangements						•	•	•			•										•	
Payments arrears				•	•		•				•	•										
Controls on payments for invisible transactions and current transfers	•						•	•		•	•		•	•		•	•				•	
Proceeds from exports and/or invisible transactions Repatriation requirements					•					•	•		•	•			•				•	
Surrender requirements					•					•	•		•	•			•				•	
Capital Transactions Controls on: *Capital market securities*	•	•		•	•	•	•	•	•	•	•	•	•		•	•	•		•	•	•	•
Money market instruments	•					•		•	•	•	•	•			•	•			•	•	•	•
Collective investment securities	•			•	•	•	•	•	•	•	–				•	•			•	•	•	•
Derivatives and other instruments	•			–				•	•	■	–				•	•	■			•	•	•
Commercial credits	•			•	•		•			•	•		•				•					
Financial credits	•			•	•		•			•	•		•				•	•			•	•
Guarantees, sureties, and financial backup facilities				•	•	•	•			■	–		•	•			■					
Direct investment	•	•	•	•	•	•		•	•	•	•	•	•		•	•	•		•	•	•	•
Liquidation of direct investment	•									•		•	•				•					
Real estate transactions	•		•		•					•		•	•	•			•		•	•	•	•
Personal capital transactions	•				•					•	•	•	•									
Provisions specific to: *Commercial banks and other credit institutions*	•	•		•	•	•	•	•	•	•	•	•	•	•	•	•	•	•	•		•	
Institutional investors	•	•	•	•	•	•	•	•	•	•	–	•	•		•	•	•	•	•	•	•	•

Summary Features of Exchange Arrangements and Regulatory Frameworks for Current and Capital Transactions in IMF Member Countries
(As of date shown on first country page; symbol key at end of table)

	Grenada	Guatemala	Guinea	Guinea-Bissau	Guyana	Haiti	Honduras	Hungary	Iceland	India	Indonesia	Iran	Iraq	Ireland	Israel	Italy	Jamaica	Japan	Jordan	Kazakhstan	Kenya	Kiribati
Status under IMF Articles of Agreement Article VIII	•	•	•	•	•	•	•	•	•	•	•	•		•	•	•	•	•	•	•	•	•
Article XIV													•									
Exchange Rate Arrangements																						
No separate legal tender																						✚
Currency board	◊																					
Conventional peg				▲															◊			
Stabilized arrangement					◊							◊										
Crawling peg																						
Crawl-like arrangement						◊	◊										◊			◊		
Pegged exchange rate within horizontal bands																						
Other managed arrangement			•									*										
Floating		•						•	•	•	•										•	
Free floating														⊕	•	⊕		•				
Exchange rate structure Dual exchange rates			•																			
Multiple exchange rates												•										
Arrangements for Payments and Receipts Bilateral payments arrangements		•			•		•		•				•					•				
Payments arrears			•	•					•				•									
Controls on payments for invisible transactions and current transfers	•		•	•			•		•		•	•						•		•		
Proceeds from exports and/or invisible transactions Repatriation requirements	•		•				•		•	•	•										•	■
Surrender requirements	•		•				•		•													
Capital Transactions Controls on: *Capital market securities*	•		•	•			•	•	•	•	•	•	•		•		•	•		•	•	•
Money market instruments	•		•	•			•	•	•	•	•	•	•				•	•		•	•	•
Collective investment securities	•		•	•			•	•	•	•	•	•	•			•	•	•		•	•	•
Derivatives and other instruments	•		•	•				•	•	•	•	–	•		•		•	•		•	•	•
Commercial credits	•		•	•	•		•	•		•	•	•					•			•		■
Financial credits	•		•	•	•		•	•	•	•	•	•	•				•	•		•		•
Guarantees, sureties, and financial backup facilities			•	•	•		•	•	•	•	•	•					•			•		•
Direct investment	•						•	•	•	•	•	•	•	•	•	•	•	•	•	•	•	•
Liquidation of direct investment	•							•	•	•	•	•	•				•					■
Real estate transactions	•		•	•			•	•	•	•	•	•		•			•	•	•		•	■
Personal capital transactions	•		•	•					•	•		•	•				•			•		■
Provisions specific to: *Commercial banks and other credit institutions*	•	•	•	•	•	•	•	•	•	•	•	•				•	•	•		•	•	■
Institutional investors		•	–	•	–		•	•	•	•	•	–				•	•	•	•	•	•	–

Summary Features of Exchange Arrangements and Regulatory Frameworks for Current and Capital Transactions in IMF Member Countries

(As of date shown on first page of country chapter; symbol key at end of table)

	Korea	Kosovo	Kuwait	Kyrgyz Republic	Lao People's Dem. Rep.	Latvia	Lebanon	Lesotho	Liberia	Libya	Lithuania	Luxembourg	FYR Macedonia	Madagascar	Malawi	Malaysia	Maldives	Mali	Malta	Marshall Islands	Mauritania	Mauritius
Status under IMF Articles of Agreement Article VIII	•		•	•	•	•	•	•		•	•	•	•	•	•	•		•	•	•	•	•
Article XIV		•							•								•					
Exchange Rate Arrangements																						
No separate legal tender		▲																		◊		
Currency board											❖											
Conventional peg			*			❖		✚		○								▲				
Stabilized arrangement					◊		◊						▲				◊					
Crawling peg																						
Crawl-like arrangement																						
Pegged exchange rate within horizontal bands																						
Other managed arrangement				•					◊					•	•						•	
Floating	•															•						•
Free floating												⊕							⊕			
Exchange rate structure Dual exchange rates				•										•	•		•					
Multiple exchange rates																						
Arrangements for Payments and Receipts Bilateral payments arrangements				•	•					•			•	•							•	
Payments arrears				•	−				•													
Controls on payments for invisible transactions and current transfers		•	•	•			•			•		•		•	•			•			•	
Proceeds from exports and/or invisible transactions Repatriation requirements	•			•				•		•				•	•			•				
Surrender requirements				•				•		•				•			•					
Capital Transactions Controls on: *Capital market securities*	•	•	•	•	•		•	•		•	•	•	•	•	•	•		•	•	−	•	•
Money market instruments			•	•	•		•	•		•	•	•	•	•	•	•		•		−	•	•
Collective investment securities			•	•	•		•	•		•	•	•	•	•	•	•		•		−	■	•
Derivatives and other instruments			•	■			•	■		■	•	•	•	•		■		•		−	■	
Commercial credits				•	•		•	•						•	•		•			−		
Financial credits				•	•		•	•		•				•	•	•		•		−	•	
Guarantees, sureties, and financial backup facilities							•			•				•	•	•		•		−	•	
Direct investment	•		•	•	•		•	•		•	•	•	•	•	•	•		•	•		•	•
Liquidation of direct investment										•				•						−		
Real estate transactions			•	•	•	•	•	•		•	•	•	•	•	•	•	•	•	•	•	•	•
Personal capital transactions				•				•		•	•			•	•	•	•	•		−		
Provisions specific to: *Commercial banks and other credit institutions*	•	•	•	•	•	•	•	•	•	•			•	•	•	•	•	•		−	•	•
Institutional investors	•	•		•	−		•	•	•	•	•	−		•	•	•		•	•	•	−	•

	Mexico	Micronesia	Moldova	Mongolia	Montenegro	Morocco	Mozambique	Myanmar	Namibia	Nepal	Netherlands	New Zealand	Nicaragua	Niger	Nigeria	Norway	Oman	Pakistan	Palau	Panama	Papua New Guinea	Paraguay
Status under IMF Articles of Agreement Article VIII	●	●	●	●	●	●	●		●	●	●	●	●	●		●	●	●	●	●	●	●
Article XIV								●							●							
Exchange Rate Arrangements																						
No separate legal tender		◇			▲														◇	◇		
Currency board																						
Conventional peg						*			+	+				▲			◇					
Stabilized arrangement																						
Crawling peg													◇									
Crawl-like arrangement																						
Pegged exchange rate within horizontal bands																						
Other managed arrangement							●								●							●
Floating			●	●		●						●						●			●	
Free floating	●										⊕					●						
Exchange rate structure Dual exchange rates								●														
Multiple exchange rates			●												●							
Arrangements for Payments and Receipts Bilateral payments arrangements	●		●	●			●						●								●	
Payments arrears			●				●						●									
Controls on payments for invisible transactions and current transfers		●		●	●	●	●	●	●	●				●	●			●			●	●
Proceeds from exports and/or invisible transactions Repatriation requirements		●				●	●	●	●	●				●	●			●				
Surrender requirements						●	●		●	●				●	●			●				
Capital Transactions Controls on: *Capital market securities*	●	●	●	●	●	●	●	●	●	●		●		●	●	●	●	●				●
Money market instruments	●	■	●		●	●	●	●	●	●				●	●			●				●
Collective investment securities	●		●			●	●	●	●	●				●				●				
Derivatives and other instruments	●		●			●	●		●					●			●	●				●
Commercial credits		■	●			●	●		●	●			●	●	●			●				
Financial credits	●	■	●			●	●		●	●			●	●	●			●				
Guarantees, sureties, and financial backup facilities	●	■	●			●	●	●	●	●				●				●			●	●
Direct investment	●	●				●	●		●	●	●	●		●		●	●	●	●			
Liquidation of direct investment			●				●	●		●				●	●							
Real estate transactions	●	●	●	●	●	●	●	●	●	●			●	●		●	●	●	●			●
Personal capital transactions	●	■	●	●		●	●	●	●	●			●	●	●	●		●				
Provisions specific to: *Commercial banks and other credit institutions*	●	●	●		●	●	●	●	●	●			●	●	●	●	●	●			●	●
Institutional investors	●	–	●	–	●	●	●	–	●	●		●	●	●	–	●	–	●	●		●	●

Summary Features of Exchange Arrangements and Regulatory Frameworks for Current and Capital Transactions in IMF Member Countries

(As of date shown on first page of country chapter; symbol key at end of table)

	Peru	Philippines	Poland	Portugal	Qatar	Romania	Russia	Rwanda	Samoa	San Marino	São Tomé and Príncipe	Saudi Arabia	Senegal	Serbia	Seychelles	Sierra Leone	Singapore	Slovak Republic	Slovenia	Solomon Islands	Somalia	South Africa
Status under IMF Articles of Agreement Article VIII	•	•	•	•	•	•	•	•	•	•		•	•	•	•	•	•	•	•	•		•
Article XIV											•										•	
Exchange Rate Arrangements																						
No separate legal tender										▲												
Currency board																						
Conventional peg					◊				*		▲	◊	▲							*		
Stabilized arrangement																						
Crawling peg																						
Crawl-like arrangement							◊										*					
Pegged exchange rate within horizontal bands																						
Other managed arrangement							•															
Floating	•	•				•									•	•	•					•
Free floating			•	⊕														⊕	⊕		•	
Exchange rate structure Dual exchange rates																					•	
Multiple exchange rates																•						
Arrangements for Payments and Receipts Bilateral payments arrangements	•	•	•		•	•	•				•		•	•					•	•	−	
Payments arrears											•				•	•					−	
Controls on payments for invisible transactions and current transfers		•	•					•	•				•	•	•		•		•		•	•
Proceeds from exports and/or invisible transactions Repatriation requirements		•					•		•				•	•	•					•		•
Surrender requirements		•							•				•							•		•
Capital Transactions Controls on: *Capital market securities*		•	•	•			•		•	•		•	•	•		•		•	•			•
Money market instruments		•	•				•		•	•		•	•	•		•			•	•		•
Collective investment securities		•	•	•			•		•	•		•	•	•		•		•	•		−	•
Derivatives and other instruments	•	•	•		•					•		•	•	•				■	•	•	−	•
Commercial credits		•	•						•	−		•	•									•
Financial credits		•	•							•	•	−		•		•			•	•		•
Guarantees, sureties, and financial backup facilities		•									−	•	•	•		•				•		•
Direct investment		•	•	•		•			•	•		•	•	•		•		•	•	•		•
Liquidation of direct investment									•					•						•		
Real estate transactions		•	•	•	•	•			•	•	•	•	•	•	•	•	•	•	•	•		•
Personal capital transactions		•	•		•				•	•		•		•		•				•	−	•
Provisions specific to: *Commercial banks and other credit institutions*	•	•	•	•	•	•	•	•	•	•	•	•	•	•	•	•	•	•	•	•	−	•
Institutional investors	•	•	•	•	•	•			•	•	−	•	•	•	•	•		•	•	•	−	•

Summary Features of Exchange Arrangements and Regulatory Frameworks for Current and Capital Transactions in IMF Member Countries
(As of date shown on first country page; symbol key at end of table)

	South Sudan	Spain	Sri Lanka	St. Kitts and Nevis	St. Lucia	St. Vincent and the Grenadines	Sudan	Suriname	Swaziland	Sweden	Switzerland	Syria	Tajikistan	Tanzania	Thailand	Timor-Leste	Togo	Tonga	Trinidad and Tobago	Tunisia	Turkey	Turkmenistan
Status under IMF Articles of Agreement Article VIII		•	•	•	•	•	•	•	•	•	•		•	•	•	•	•	•	•	•	•	
Article XIV	•											•										•
Exchange Rate Arrangements																						
No separate legal tender																◊						
Currency board				◊	◊	◊																
Conventional peg	◊								✚								▲					◊
Stabilized arrangement								◊					◊							◊		
Crawling peg																						
Crawl-like arrangement																					*	
Pegged exchange rate within horizontal bands																		*				
Other managed arrangement								•			•	*										
Floating			•											•	•						•	
Free floating		⊕								•												
Exchange rate structure Dual exchange rates								•				•										
Multiple exchange rates							•															
Arrangements for Payments and Receipts Bilateral payments arrangements	−							•					•	•							•	•
Payments arrears	−												•									
Controls on payments for invisible transactions and current transfers	−		•	•	•	•	•	•	•				•	•	•		•	•		•	•	•
Proceeds from exports and/or invisible transactions Repatriation requirements	−		•		•	•	•		•				•	•	•		•			•		•
Surrender requirements	−		•		•				•				•				•			•		•
Capital Transactions Controls on: *Capital market securities*	−	•	•	•	•	•	•	•	•	•	•	•	•	•	•		•	•	•	•	•	•
Money market instruments	−	•	•	•	•	•	•	•	•	•	•	•	•	•	•		•	•	•	•	•	•
Collective investment securities	−	•	•	•	•	•	■	•	•	•	•	•	•	•	•		•	•		•	•	•
Derivatives and other instruments	−	•	•	■	•		■	•	•	•	•	•	•	•	•		•	•		•	•	•
Commercial credits	−		•	•	•		•					•	•				•			•	•	•
Financial credits	−	•	•	•	•	•		•	•	•	•	•	•	•			•			•	•	•
Guarantees, sureties, and financial backup facilities	−			•	•		•	•				•		•			•			•		•
Direct investment	−	•	•	•	•		•	•	•	•	•	•	•	•	•		•	•	•	•	•	•
Liquidation of direct investment	−		•	−				•					•	•					•			•
Real estate transactions	−	•	•	•	•		•	•	•	•	•	•	•	•	•	•	•	•	•	•	•	•
Personal capital transactions	−		•	•	•	•	•	•				•	•	•	•		•	•		•		•
Provisions specific to: *Commercial banks and other credit institutions*	−	•	•	•	•	•	•	•	•	•	•	•	•	•	•		•	•	•	•	•	•
Institutional investors	−	•	•	•	•	•	•	•	•	•	•	−		•	•	−	•		•	•	•	•

Summary Features of Exchange Arrangements and Regulatory Frameworks for Current and Capital Transactions in IMF Member Countries
(As of date shown on first page of country chapter; symbol key at end of table)

	Tuvalu	Uganda	Ukraine	United Arab Emirates	United Kingdom	United States	Uruguay	Uzbekistan	Vanuatu	Venezuela	Vietnam	Yemen	Zambia	Zimbabwe	Aruba	Hong Kong SAR	Curaçao and Sint Maarten
Status under IMF Articles of Agreement																	
Article VIII		•	•	•	•	•	•	•	•	•	•	•	•	•	•	•	•
Article XIV	•																
Exchange Rate Arrangements																	
No separate legal tender	+													◊			
Currency board																◊	
Conventional peg				◊						◊					◊		◊
Stabilized arrangement			◊								◊	◊					
Crawling peg																	
Crawl-like arrangement								◊									
Pegged exchange rate within horizontal bands																	
Other managed arrangement									*								
Floating		•					•						•				
Free floating					•	•											
Exchange rate structure																	
Dual exchange rates			•							•							
Multiple exchange rates								•									
Arrangements for Payments and Receipts																	
Bilateral payments arrangements	−	•	•				•	•	■	•	•			•			
Payments arrears	−	•							■			•	•				
Controls on payments for invisible transactions and current transfers	−		•					•		•					•		•
Proceeds from exports and/or invisible transactions																	
Repatriation requirements	−		•					•	■	•	•		•		•		
Surrender requirements	−		•					•	■	•					•		
Capital Transactions																	
Controls on:																	
Capital market securities	−	•	•				•	•	■	•				•	•		•
Money market instruments	−	•					•	•	■	•				•	•		•
Collective investment securities	−	•	•				•	•	■	•				•	•		•
Derivatives and other instruments	−	•					•		■	■				•	•	•	•
Commercial credits	−	•					•	•	■	•				•	•		•
Financial credits	−	•					•	•	■	•	•	•		•	•		•
Guarantees, sureties, and financial backup facilities	−	•					•	•	■	•				•	•		•
Direct investment	−	•	•	•			•	•	■	•	•			•	•		•
Liquidation of direct investment	−	•					•	•	■	•				•	•		•
Real estate transactions	−	•	•	•			•	•	■	•				•	•		•
Personal capital transactions	−	•					•	•	■	•	•			•	•		•
Provisions specific to:																	
Commercial banks and other credit institutions	−	•	•	•	•		•	•	■	•	•			•	•	•	•
Institutional investors	−	•	−		•	•	•	•	■	•	•	•		•	•	•	•

Key

• Indicates that the specified practice is a feature of the exchange system.

− Indicates that data were not available at the time of publication.

■ Indicates that the specified practice is not regulated.

⊕ Indicates that the country participates in the euro area.

❖ Indicates that the country participates in the European Exchange Rate Mechanism (ERM II).

◊ Indicates that flexibility is limited vis-à-vis the U.S. dollar.

▲ Indicates that flexibility is limited vis-à-vis the euro.

+ Indicates that flexibility is limited vis-à-vis another single currency.

○ Indicates that flexibility is limited vis-à-vis the SDR.

* Indicates that flexibility is limited vis-à-vis another basket of currencies.

Country Table Matrix

Status under IMF Articles of Agreement

Article VIII
Article XIV

Exchange Measures

Restrictions and/or multiple currency practices

Exchange measures imposed for security reasons

In accordance with IMF Executive Board Decision No. 144-(52/51)

Other security restrictions

References to legal instruments and hyperlinks

Exchange Arrangement

Currency

Other legal tender

Exchange rate structure

Unitary

Dual

Multiple

Classification

No separate legal tender

Currency board

Conventional peg

Stabilized arrangement

Crawling peg

Crawl-like arrangement

Pegged exchange rate within horizontal bands

Other managed arrangement

Floating

Free floating

Official exchange rate

Monetary policy framework

Exchange rate anchor

Monetary aggregate target

Inflation-targeting framework

Other monetary framework

Exchange tax

Exchange subsidy

Foreign exchange market

Spot exchange market

Operated by the central bank

Foreign exchange standing facility

Allocation

Auction

Fixing

Interbank market

Over the counter

Brokerage

Market making

Forward exchange market

Official cover of forward operations

References to legal instruments and hyperlinks

Arrangements for Payments and Receipts

Prescription of currency requirements

Controls on the use of domestic currency

For current transactions and payments

For capital transactions

Transactions in capital and money market instruments

Transactions in derivatives and other instruments

Credit operations

Use of foreign exchange among residents

Payments arrangements

Bilateral payments arrangements

Operative

Inoperative

Regional arrangements

Clearing agreements

Barter agreements and open accounts

Administration of control

Payments arrears

Official

Private

Controls on trade in gold (coins and/or bullion)

On domestic ownership and/or trade

On external trade

Controls on exports and imports of banknotes

On exports

Domestic currency

Foreign currency

On imports

Domestic currency

Foreign currency

References to legal instruments and hyperlinks

Resident Accounts

Foreign exchange accounts permitted

Held domestically

Approval required

Held abroad

Approval required

Accounts in domestic currency held abroad

Accounts in domestic currency convertible into foreign currency

References to legal instruments and hyperlinks

Nonresident Accounts

Foreign exchange accounts permitted

Approval required

Domestic currency accounts

Convertible into foreign currency

Approval required

Blocked accounts

References to legal instruments and hyperlinks

Imports and Import Payments

Foreign exchange budget

Financing requirements for imports

Minimum financing requirements

Advance payment requirements

Advance import deposits

Documentation requirements for release of foreign exchange for imports

Domiciliation requirements

Preshipment inspection

Letters of credit

Import licenses used as exchange licenses

Other

Import licenses and other nontariff measures

Positive list

Negative list

Open general licenses

Licenses with quotas

Other nontariff measures

Import taxes and/or tariffs

Taxes collected through the exchange system

State import monopoly

References to legal instruments and hyperlinks

Exports and Export Proceeds

Repatriation requirements

Surrender requirements

Surrender to the central bank

Surrender to authorized dealers

Financing requirements

Documentation requirements

Letters of credit

Guarantees

Domiciliation

Preshipment inspection

Other

Export licenses

Without quotas

With quotas

Export taxes

Collected through the exchange system

Other export taxes

References to legal instruments and hyperlinks

Payments for Invisible Transactions and Current Transfers

Controls on these transfers

Trade-related payments

Prior approval

Quantitative limits

Indicative limits/bona fide test

Investment-related payments

Prior approval

Quantitative limits

Indicative limits/bona fide test

Payments for travel

Prior approval

Quantitative limits

Indicative limits/bona fide test

Personal payments

Prior approval

Quantitative limits

Indicative limits/bona fide test

Foreign workers' wages

Prior approval

Quantitative limits

Indicative limits/bona fide test

Credit card use abroad

Prior approval

Quantitative limits

Indicative limits/bona fide test

Other payments

Prior approval

Quantitative limits

Indicative limits/bona fide test

References to legal instruments and hyperlinks

Proceeds from Invisible Transactions and Current Transfers

Repatriation requirements

Surrender requirements

Surrender to the central bank

Surrender to authorized dealers

Restrictions on use of funds

References to legal instruments and hyperlinks

Capital Transactions

Controls on capital transactions

Repatriation requirements

Surrender requirements

Surrender to the central bank

Surrender to authorized dealers

Controls on capital and money market instruments

On capital market securities

Shares or other securities of a participating nature

Purchase locally by nonresidents

Sale or issue locally by nonresidents

Purchase abroad by residents

Sale or issue abroad by residents

Bonds or other debt securities

Purchase locally by nonresidents

Sale or issue locally by nonresidents

Purchase abroad by residents

Sale or issue abroad by residents

On money market instruments

Purchase locally by nonresidents

Sale or issue locally by nonresidents

Purchase abroad by residents

Sale or issue abroad by residents

On collective investment securities

Purchase locally by nonresidents

Sale or issue locally by nonresidents

Purchase abroad by residents

Sale or issue abroad by residents

Controls on derivatives and other instruments

Purchase locally by nonresidents

Sale or issue locally by nonresidents

Purchase abroad by residents

Sale or issue abroad by residents

Controls on credit operations

Commercial credits

By residents to nonresidents

To residents from nonresidents

Financial credits

By residents to nonresidents

To residents from nonresidents

Guarantees, sureties, and financial backup facilities

By residents to nonresidents

To residents from nonresidents

Controls on direct investment

Outward direct investment

Inward direct investment

Controls on liquidation of direct investment

Controls on real estate transactions

Purchase abroad by residents

Purchase locally by nonresidents

Sale locally by nonresidents

Controls on personal capital transactions

Loans

By residents to nonresidents

To residents from nonresidents

Gifts, endowments, inheritances, and legacies

By residents to nonresidents

To residents from nonresidents

Settlement of debts abroad by immigrants

Transfer of assets

Transfer abroad by emigrants

Transfer into the country by immigrants

Transfer of gambling and prize earnings

References to legal instruments and hyperlinks

Provisions Specific to the Financial Sector

Provisions specific to commercial banks and other credit institutions

Borrowing abroad

Maintenance of accounts abroad

Lending to nonresidents (financial or commercial credits)

Lending locally in foreign exchange

Purchase of locally issued securities denominated in foreign exchange

Differential treatment of deposit accounts in foreign exchange

Reserve requirements

Liquid asset requirements

Interest rate controls

Credit controls

Differential treatment of deposit accounts held by nonresidents

Reserve requirements

Liquid asset requirements

Interest rate controls

Credit controls

Investment regulations

Abroad by banks

In banks by nonresidents

Open foreign exchange position limits

On resident assets and liabilities

On nonresident assets and liabilities

Provisions specific to institutional investors

Insurance companies

Limits (max.) on securities issued by nonresidents

Limits (max.) on investment portfolio held abroad

Limits (min.) on investment portfolio held locally

Currency-matching regulations on assets/liabilities composition

Pension funds

Limits (max.) on securities issued by nonresidents

Limits (max.) on investment portfolio held abroad

 Limits (min.) on investment portfolio held locally

 Currency-matching regulations on assets/liabilities composition

Investment firms and collective investment funds

 Limits (max.) on securities issued by nonresidents

 Limits (max.) on investment portfolio held abroad

 Limits (min.) on investment portfolio held locally

 Currency-matching regulations on assets/liabilities composition

References to legal instruments and hyperlinks

Changes during 2012

Status under IMF Articles of Agreement

Exchange measures

Exchange arrangement

Arrangements for payments and receipts

Resident accounts

Nonresident accounts

Imports and import payments

Exports and export proceeds

Payments for invisible transactions and current transfers

Proceeds from invisible transactions and current transfers

Capital transactions

Controls on capital and money market instruments

Controls on derivatives and other instruments

Controls on credit operations

Controls on direct investment

Controls on liquidation of direct investment

Controls on real estate transactions

Controls on personal capital transactions

Provisions specific to the financial sector

Provisions specific to commercial banks and other credit institutions

Provisions specific to institutional investors

Changes during 2013

Status under IMF Articles of Agreement

Exchange measures

Exchange arrangement

Arrangements for payments and receipts

Resident accounts

Nonresident accounts

Imports and import payments

Exports and export proceeds

Payments for invisible transactions and current transfers

Proceeds from invisible transactions and current transfers

Capital transactions

Controls on capital and money market instruments

Controls on derivatives and other instruments

Controls on credit operations

Controls on direct investment

Controls on liquidation of direct investment

Controls on real estate transactions

Controls on personal capital transactions

Provisions specific to the financial sector

Provisions specific to commercial banks and other credit institutions

Provisions specific to institutional investors